What's Worth Teaching?

SUNY Series in Philosophy of Education
Philip L. Smith, Editor

What's Worth Teaching?

Selecting, Organizing, and Integrating Knowledge

MARION BRADY

State University of New York Press

Published by
State University of New York Press, Albany

Printed in the United States of America

For information, address State University of New York
Press, State University Plaza, Albany, N.Y., 12246

Library of Congress Cataloging in Publication Data

Brady, Marion, 1927-
    What's worth teaching?

    (SUNY series in philosophy of education)
    Includes index.
    1. Education—United States—Curricula.
2. Curriculum evaluation—United States. 3. Curriculum
planning—United States. I. Title
LB1570.B744   1988   375'.001'0973   87-33636
ISBN 0-88706-815-4
ISBN 0-88706-816-2 (pbk.)

10   9   8   7   6   5   4

Written approval to reprint this book was granted by Suny Press, July, 1993.
Marion Brady's *What's Worth Teaching? Selecting, Organizing, and Integrating
Knowledge* published by the State University of New York Press ©1989 by the
Board of Trustees of State University of New York.

Contents

Introduction

"Why do we keep our heads covered and always wear a little prayer shawl?" "Why does the master have the final word at home?" "Why are the brides chosen for sons, and daughters taught to mend and tend?" In *Fiddler on the Roof,* Tevya questions why the people of his little village follow certain customs. He then explains: "Tradition." What is done is done because that is the way it has always been done. Period.

Those committed to the general education curriculum offered by most American schools and universities are likely to give explanations of current practice only a little more satisfactory than that provided by Tevya. What we teach is determined primarily by what has been taught. The assumed validity of the content of traditional education stems largely from a powerful assumption: if one knows something, and most other well-educated people also know it, then it must be worth knowing and should be taught to the next generation.

There is abundant evidence that the traditional general education curriculum is not doing the job. Earnest Boyer: "The undergraduate curriculum is a disaster area." Harlan Cleveland: "It is a well-known scandal that our whole educational system is geared more to categorizing and analyzing patches of knowledge than to threading them together." Robert Stevens: "We have lost sight of our responsibility for synthesizing learning." Neil Postman: "There is no longer any principle that unifies the school curriculum and furnishes it with meaning." John Goodlad; "What students are asked to relate to in school [is] increasingly artificial, cut off from the human experiences subject matter is supposed to reflect."

Within individual academic disciplines, there is no less criticism. Greg Stefanich and Charles Dedrick: "Mathematics and science education in America's schools is sorely defective." Paul DeHart Hurd: "Biology, chemistry, physics and earth science . . . no longer exist as they are portrayed in the simple division of school science into subjects." Philip Curtin: "Historians are narrower in their knowledge and understanding than they have ever been."

Perceptive observers are insisting that much that students need to know they are not being taught, and much that students *are* learning is a waste of time and money. The traditional curriculum is tolerated primarily because what

1

is being taught is no longer considered particularly important. What really matters are the symbols—the grades, certificates, degrees, and titles. There is little demand (except by industries interested in the schools doing specialized training for them) that education bear a demonstrable relationship to real problems, situations, and needs.

To the casual observer it may appear that we educators are aware of our problems and are attempting to deal with them. In the last decade or two, we have tried flexible scheduling, open schools, longer school days, team teaching, computer technology, middle schools, programmed instruction, diagnostic testing, lengthened school terms, ability grouping, and a variety of other educational innovations. What could escape notice, however, is that almost all the activity has been *administrative* in nature. Innovations have altered various aspects of the delivery system, but the intellectual content and organization of that which is delivered has remained basically unchanged since the nineteenth century.

The problems with the curriculum that critics were discussing before the turn of the century are still with us, most of them more serious than ever. Information is growing exponentially, yet we still have no objective criteria to guide our decisions about what to teach. Learning theorists insist that teaching for understanding requires the building of conceptual structures, but we hardly know what they mean. We know that certain very powerful ideas should be introduced early and developed year after year, but we make almost no provision for doing so. Great thinkers have said for centuries that everything is related to everything else, yet we organize instruction so as to send just the opposite message. It takes no more than a moment's thought to verify that almost everything worth knowing is too complex to test, yet we are increasingly gearing instruction to match our crude ability to measure.

Earnest Boyer is right. The general education curriculum is a disaster area.

A long time ago, general education missed the path. Dazzled by the rewards of specialization in industry and other areas of life, it seemed appropriate to adopt a similar approach to the instruction of the young. There is, of course, a place for specialization. The student with mathematical ability ought to be helped to develop that ability to the utmost. The same should be done for the student of history, language, music, or automatic transmissions. But some of this and some of that, no matter how carefully selected cannot a coherent curriculum make, cannot provide an educational experience that welds language, mathematics, the social sciences, the humanities, and the natural sciences into a mutually supportive, logical, conceptually unified whole.

The problems are fundamental. They cannot be solved with any sort of mandated multidisciplinary or interdisciplinary mix of subjects or courses, cannot be solved by focusing on selected topics or "universal human problems," cannot be solved by making philosophy or some other discipline the core of the curriculum, cannot be solved by institutional reorganization.

But the problems can be solved. I offer as a basis for solution an approach based on two propositions. The first is the lesson taught by Galileo's and Descartes's contention that knowledge is nothing more nor less than the power to manipulate the world according to the principles inherent in the model used to represent it. The second is summarized by Stephen Jay Gould's observation in *The Panda's Thumb* that "information always reaches us through the strong filters of culture, hope and expectation."

I will argue that the primary objective of general education is to expand our understanding of reality; that in our attempt to understand reality, our perceptions are structured by our differing native sociocultural systems; that these differing systems must therefore be understood, a task necessitating the use of a conceptual model; and that such a model, if it is comprehensive, will reflect our present level of understanding of the "sociocultural screen" through which we view reality, and reality itself, and will serve as a relatively simple and practical tool for selecting, organizing, integrating, and expanding the content of instruction bearing on reality.

This is not a familiar idea in education. The traditional view is that the curriculum derives from the needs of learners, the problems of society, the content of the academic disciplines, or some variation or combination of the three. These are all valid sources of curriculum content, and there will be passages in this discussion which are supportive of them. But those who try, on the basis of a sentence here or a paragraph there, to bend the basic proposition herein advanced to make it fit within the bounds of Parker, Counts, Dewey, or other curriculum theorists will almost certainly find the argument impossible to follow, or will join in the conclusion of one reviewer that what is being said "borders on being pure schlock."

It may seem presumptuous to advance a theory of curriculum and make almost no reference to the massive literature on the subject. We tend to assume that new insights come from piling up existing knowledge and gaining a fresh view from the elevation supposedly thus provided. That is not the process that led to my conclusion that a formal model of the concept of culture provides a structure for the curriculum. The idea is not an extension or elaboration of the work of those considered to be the major thinkers in the field of curriculum design. There seems little reason, therefore, to restate their positions or to argue the relative merit of those positions.

If there is an identifiable "father" of this central thesis, it is David Potter, under whom the author studied when Potter was chairman of American studies at Yale. The idea was not his, but Potter raised the broad questions which led to its eventual development. Carroll Quigley, professor of history at Georgetown University's School for Foreign Service; Robert Redfield, chairman of the Department of Anthropology at the University of Chicago; a year or so of conversations with Alvin Toffler and Michael McDanield discussing a possible joint project under the sponsorship of Prentice-Hall; and Howard Brady, the author's brother and collaborator on other books and projects, were also major sources. Letters of support in response to an article by the author published in the *Phi Delta Kappan* in October of 1966 played a role. The article outlined the basic ideas which are herein presented in greater detail.

Although well over half the book is devoted to a discussion and illustration of the kind of content likely to grow out of a curriculum structured by a formal model of the concept of culture, no attempt will be made to lay out a complete sequence of instruction. Neither will much be said about procedures for implementing new curricula, about the present near impossibility of significant curricular change, or about prior or alternative efforts to create a more coherent curriculum. Those matters are beyond the scope of this intentionally lean book.

I have but a single purpose: to outline a new theoretical base for the general education curriculum. I want to show that, in general education's pursuit of an understanding of reality, a formal model for the study of the concept of culture is the most powerful tool available. I will maintain that such a model can encompass all knowledge, suggest new disciplines, identify areas of study now neglected, indicate the content most appropriate for general education, suggest relative degrees of content significance, organize content logically, provide students with conceptual structure, integrate every part of the curriculum with every other part, and furnish mechanisms by means of which knowledge can be systematically expanded.

These are, admittedly, extravagant-sounding claims. The centrality of the concept of culture in a curriculum dedicated to expanding an understanding of reality is as yet generally unappreciated and unexplored. I will try to suggest its enormous promise, and give at least a glimpse of the potential power and elegance of a general education curriculum built upon it.

Chapter 1

Selecting Knowledge

The Problems

Spring Road Estates. Whispering Hill Houses. Heslop Homes. Brookwood Manor. Levitt Park...

In the years following World War II, the modern subdivision was invented. Bulldozers leveled hundreds of thousands of acres, and crews moved in to mass-produce new houses for millions of Americans. Returning military veterans acquired government-guaranteed loans and bought homes in the subdivisions. They were joined by apartment dwellers from the cities who had "always wanted a little place of their own." Other neighbors came as part of a general exodus from rural areas.

As a cultural phenomenon, the subdivision was significant. Locations chosen for tract housing frequently created a variety of stresses on local tax structures. Narrow price ranges populated housing developments with families of similar income, social class, and age. Truck farms which had once been sources of food were often taken over as building sites. Construction costs dictated street and sewer layouts, determined the physical relationship of houses, and thereby structured to a degree the interactions of inhabitants. Cost considerations shaped the houses themselves in ways which subtly programmed certain kinds of family life and neighboring. Commercial areas changed location and older neighborhoods changed character in response to subdivision growth.

The social, political, and economic effects of the suburbanization movement in America during the third quarter of the twentieth century were nothing less than revolutionary. No one can understand where America has been the last several decades, where it now is, or where it is likely to go without understanding this vast movement.

Where does one acquire the complex of concepts essential to the exploration of this revolution?

Not in the schools.

To Americans, *individualism* is a very positive word. It is often combined with *rugged.* Rugged individualists, it is believed, conquered the frontier, established the nation, put it on a solid philosophical footing, organized the Industrial Revolution, made American business preeminent, gave the United States a technological edge, established it as a world power, saw the nation through difficult times, and, if given free rein by those in power, will do so again. Most of America's heroes have been perceived as rugged individualists.

The emphasis on individualism obscures the fact that most personal needs are met, most problems are solved, most public goals are attained by *organized, collective* action. *Organizations* acquire and wield power, produce goods, and direct social change. *Organizations* manage the economy, protect life and property, and cushion the cost of accidents and illness. *Organizations* structure religious worship, design recreation, produce the messages the media transmit, and direct the education of the young. Security, stability, a sense of worth and accomplishment, and assurance that others care—even these kinds of deep psychological needs are met primarily by *organizations.*

The quality of our lives is largely determined by the quality of the political, economic, social, and religious organizations which structure them. One would suppose, therefore, that expanding our understanding of human organizations would be a major objective of general education. Surely it is important to understand why and how organizations appear and the variety of forms they take. It would certainly seem important that we understand why some organizations are productive and others are not, why so few are self-renewing, and how all can be made more responsive to human need. It would seem important that we learn why some organizations function with a minimum of internal friction, but others are continuously wracked by conflict and dissension.

Where does one acquire the concepts essential to an understanding of these entities which play so large a role in our security and happiness?

Not in the schools.

In two years, five years, ten years, discussion of educational problems may be irrelevant. Education itself may be irrelevant. The price of oil, the rate of unemployment, the condition of the stock market, the incidence of violent

crime—all irrelevant. The pending promotion at work, the approaching graduation ceremony, the planned remodeling of the house, the last-minute Christmas
shopping—irrelevant. For sitting silently in silos and launch tubes, out of sight
and usually out of mind, are devices which can make almost everything
irrelevant.

If the almost unthinkable should happen, the immediate reason will not
have been a move on anyone's part to subjugate, to impose ideology, to acquire
resources, to control territory, or to destroy. The immediate cause of the last
great battle will not be greed or old-fashioned power politics, but miscalcula-
tion and misunderstanding. Afterward (if there is anyone to utter it), the most
apt phrase will be "If only we had known. . ."

There will be much that all parties ought to have known. The single most
important insight, however, will have had to do with how the mind works in situations which are tense and threatening. In any polarized relationship, defensive
activity seems essential and reasonable. Faced by an enemy, what could be more
logical than raising new fortifications, building more powerful weapons, using
stronger words to warn of one's ability to prevail? So defensive action is undertaken: the fort is strengthened, the weaponry increased, the words sharpened.

And the enemy looks across, sees the activity, and feels compelled to
improve *his* defensive capability. The fort is strengthened. Weaponry is
increased. Words are sharpened. . . In polarized situations, one's own activity
is always sincerely perceived as defensive, and the enemy's activity is always
perceived as offensive. Given those perceptions, there is no place to stop the
cycle of move and countermove. Each step up makes the next step appear more
necessary, more reasonable.

The consequences of the tendency to interpret defensive actions as offensive actions are everywhere apparent. In U.S.-Soviet relations, in the Middle
East, in Northern Ireland, in Latin America, defensive actions are being read
as offensive actions demanding defensive responses. Closer to home, the
same process leads to domestic strife, to labor-management conflict, to
neighborhood violence, to divorce, to family disorganization, to waste,
destruction, and death.

The cost of not understanding the process of polarization is incalculable.
Where will one find an attempt being made to teach the complex of concepts
central to an understanding of the process?

Not in the schools.

There is nothing particularly complex or esoteric about suburbanization
or organizational dynamics or polarization. They are the stuff of everyday life,
and a hundred or a thousand similar summaries could be written. After every

summary, the same question could be asked: where can a comprehensive understanding of this matter be gained? And an accurate response would be: not in the schools.

What *can* one learn in American schools? Much, of course, of unquestionable value. It would be difficult to bring the young together daily, put them in the company of reasonably concerned adults, provide them with space and a variety of equipment, and *not* generate experiences which were educationally defensible. Despite the demonstrable inadequacies of our educational system, most students do learn to read, learn to write well enough to get by, and learn to compute sufficiently to avoid being cheated at the checkout counter. And at least some students realize much of their potential—learn to speak a foreign language, solve difficult intellectual problems, create beautiful forms, work effectively with others, find satisfaction in an understanding of this era and the place they occupy in it, and maintain reasonable control over their own fates.

Schooling in America produces some successes, but the general education curriculum deserves very limited credit. What is taught—the actual content of the lectures, books, instructional units, films, courses, subjects, programs, and all the rest—is not a product of a comprehensive, rational theory or plan. It is not a systematic sampling of accumulated knowledge. It is not the result of a thorough, current analysis of the needs of individuals or of societies. It is not a grand design worked out by our best minds. Incredible as it may seem, American education, this vast institution which consumes so much of our wealth, time, and energy, offers the student not a coherent intellectual structure but a random heap fashioned by ancient concerns and assumptions, political expedience, accident, intellectual fads, hysteria, special interests, and myriad superficial views of the ends of education.

What, specifically, is wrong with the general education curriculum offered by our schools and colleges? There are many problems, but six are paramount.

1. *Knowledge is expanding at an every-accelerating rate, and the rapidity of social change has never been greater, yet we have no criteria for selecting what should be taught in the relatively brief instructional time available.*

If information did not expand, if new disciplines were not demanding to be recognized, if the world did not change, if our ability to deal with critically important problems were routinely exhibited, then an educational machine which pounded out the same familiar fare from one era to another would be perfectly appropriate. But the world is not static, much of what needs to be known is not in the textbooks, and no one has even begun to talk about strategies for determining what new information can safely be ignored, what must be taught, and which present content must be omitted to make room in the curriculum for changes.

An acceptable general education curriculum will be inherently dynamic and self-renewing.

2. *Our best minds tell us that all knowledge is related, yet our curriculum is fragmented and the fragments are moving farther apart.*

The traditional school subjects as now taught, and the academic disciplines from which they were derived, simply do not fit together in any coherent way. They were never *designed* to fit together. Most of our understanding of multifaceted problems, most of our awareness of relationships in the real world, has not been acquired through the use of conceptual tools developed in formal education. The thrust toward integration comes to us primarily through the media, from "synthesizers" who pay no attention to the artificial boundaries of the subjects they studied in school.

Our failure to build a coherent, unified curriculum does not stem from a lack of awareness of the problem. Well over three hundred years ago Descartes wrote, "If, therefore, anyone wishes to search out the truth of things in serious earnest, he ought not to select one special science; for all the sciences are conjoined with each other and interdependent." Herbert Spencer discussed the matter in his 1859 essay, "What Knowledge Is of Most Worth?" Before most of us were born, Alfred North Whitehead was warning the educational establishment that it needed to "eradicate the fatal disconnection of subjects which kills the vitality of the modern curriculum." Jacques Barzun said simply, "In the realm of minds as represented by great men, there is no such thing as separate, isolated subjects." Referring to higher education, Justice Felix Frankfurter wrote, "That our universities have grave shortcomings for the intellectual life of this nation is by now a commonplace. The chief source of their inadequacy is probably the curse of departmentalization." And Earnest Boyer said recently, "To dump on students the task of finding coherence in their education is indefensible."

The conclusion is inescapable. If all knowledge is related, then any curriculum in which the major elements are not related is not a good curriculum. Until students can move smoothly and logically from concept to concept and component to component, every compendium of course descriptions, every college catalog will testify to a major failure of the educational establishment—our inability to devise an educational program which reflects one of the most fundamental attributes of knowledge.

An acceptable general education curriculum will be an integrated curriculum.

3. *The learning process requires that new information become part of a coherent conceptual structure, yet no systematic attempt is being made to create a curriculum which reflects that requirement.*

The human nervous system processes and stores information in an elaborate category system. In order to make sense, new ideas have to fit within existing categories which, in turn, make sense because they fit within still more general categories.

ELECTRONICS

    CIRCUIT

        COMPON•NT

            CAPACITOR

                MOLDED MYLAR

                    3000 PICOFARADS

DRAMATIC LITERATURE

    TRAGEDY

        REALISM

            MELODRAMA

                BOUCICAULT'S THE OCTOROON

At each level within sequences such as these there are parallel entries of the same level of generality. The levels, the entries within them, and the relationships between levels and between entries are, collectively, a conceptual structure. To "understand" means to be familiar with the levels, the entries, and the relationships. To "grow in understanding" means to discover new categories, new entries within the categories, and new relationships.

For example, to the small child just beginning to form conceptual structures, every four-legged creature may be a "doggy." Soon, however, certain "dogs" become horses, other cows, still others kittens. Eventually, the label *dog* is replaced with the label *animal.* New entries are added. And, as understanding grows, each of the entries becomes itself a level with its own entries. Dogs become terriers, poodles, and spaniels—categories which are in turn elaborated even further.

There are no fundamental differences in the processes involved in understanding dogs and in understanding most of the rest of the content of general education. Education for understanding is primarily concerned with the construction, organization, and elaboration of conceptual frameworks composed of related ideas of differing levels of generality. Instruction not aimed at creating or clarifying a concept or concept relationship within such a framework ignores the mind's usual approach to processing information. Given the mind's ability to make something of almost nothing, such instruction is not necessarily a waste of time ("If you throw enough mud on the wall, some of it is bound to stick," says an old theory of pedagogy). But to leave to the student the task of figuring out how new knowledge fits together and meshes with old knowledge is an extremely inefficient approach to teaching.

Instruction which makes deliberate use of conceptual structure helps students organize knowledge. It also establishes priorities among levels of generality, helping to avoid the confusion and inefficiency which result when the trivial is mixed indiscriminately with the important. The psychology student who learns where Freud was born knows one thing. The student who knows that every human being's behavior is rational, given his or her assumptions about the situation, knows many things—knows something useful about self, neighbors, co-workers, mental patients, world leaders—about everyone. Unless the curriculum is grounded firmly in a conceptual structure, ideas which vary enormously in power will be given equal classroom time and attention, and the number of ideas which students are expected to assimilate will forever multiply.

The schools have assumed responsibility for matters other than expanding understanding. Surely, however, this is the main task, which is to say that teachers are first of all in the business of helping students build conceptual structures. An acceptable general education curriculum will be formally anchored in a single vast conceptual framework, a framework which clearly identifies important ideas, establishes their relative significance, and suggests the nature of relationships between them. Effective teachers will have this framework consciously and constantly in mind, and will consider the transfer of the structure and the fashioning of tools for its elaboration the central task of teaching.

4. *The proper subject matter of education is reality, but reality is not the focus of the general education curriculum.*

We educators assemble words about reality—about humanity, the elements, other forms of life, language, the universe, physical forces, the past—and then make the words themselves rather than that to which they refer the primary subject matter of education.

The difference between reality and words about reality is crucial—no less than the difference between listening to music and reading about it; between touching and being told about touch; between, finally, a dynamic and a dead curriculum. The teacher who says, "How does it feel to be afraid?" is probing reality. The teacher who says, "What does the author say about how it feels to be afraid?" is checking the student's memory of words on a page.

We have made a means of instruction its end. Alfred North Whitehead was unequivocal in his view of the consequences. "The secondhandedness of the learned world," he said, "is the secret of its mediocrity."

A curriculum keyed to reality always challenges, stretches abilities, moves ahead as we move toward it. It has no finite bounds, cannot be finally measured, cannot be made absolute, cannot be totally encompassed by human understanding. It keeps the teacher properly humble, demands every skill, makes clear the unavoidable subjectivity of teaching and learning, and produces results that lie far beyond our present primitive ability to evaluate.

The curriculum we have—a curriculum keyed not to reality but to what scholars say about reality—is a much simpler thing. It makes education primarily a game played with words on paper, and the winner is the student with the longest memory. A single question dominates: how much can you remember? The teaching skills required are minimal—control of the flow of words, and the recording of the number of correct and incorrect recollections of them. For that kind of work, teachers are not really necessary. The simplest of computers can manage such tasks easily.

A picture of reality is not reality. An acceptable curriculum will deal directly with reality.

5. *A defensible general education curriculum will be demonstrably applicable to daily experience.*

An acceptable curriculum will be a source of insight and a guide to action in every aspect of life—going to the supermarket, facing the prospect of death, or formulating international policy. Despite some pedantic resistance to the idea, education must be utilitarian. (Nonutilitarian education is very difficult to justify.) This does not mean, however, that education must be mundane or pedestrian. Nothing could be more "daily" than polarization, population movement, or organizational health, referred to earlier, yet those subjects are far from mundane. It is not a matter of lowering educational concern to the level of going to the supermarket, but of raising the experience of going to the supermarket to the level of significance, interest, and challenge it warrants.

6. *An acceptable general education curriculum will be universal, will be equally valid for every student.*

In every instructional situation, there will of course be differences in teaching and learning styles, in the language of instruction, in illustrative material, and much else, but the basic configuration of the curriculum will be valid for all. The concerns the curriculum addresses and the needs it will attempt to meet will transcend the particular student's age, sex, race, ethnic origin, nationality, social class, background, and life goals. It will be bound by neither time nor place, neither will it derive from peculiar contemporary or historical experience or from the assumptions or values of any one group. It will be relatively free of ethnocentrism, and, as it is refined, it will bear ever less evidence of the culture of its origin.

An acceptable general education curriculum, then, will be integrated, adaptive, self-renewing, conceptually ordered, reality based, utilitarian, and universal. In the chapters which follow, a conceptual foundation for a curriculum which meets these criteria will be described. Upon this foundation a new general education curriculum can be built.

Can be built, but almost certainly will not be. The extent of institutionalization of education makes a fundamental reworking of the curriculum one of the remotest of possibilities. If the proposition herein advanced has a positive influence on instruction, it will most likely come from its impact on individual teachers working alone in isolated classrooms.

Significant and immediate improvement in instruction is possible. All that is really necessary is for teachers to acquire the necessary conceptual framework. No institutional changes are required—no increased budgets, no new departments, no new faculty or administration, no faculty reassignment, no new courses or course titles, no professionally prepared materials, not even administrator understanding or approval. A conceptual restructuring of the general education curriculum can be accomplished by today's teachers teaching today's subjects to today's students. The theoretical basis for such a restructuring need only be understood.

In the chapters which follow, a comprehensive conceptual foundation for the general education curriculum will be described. When that foundation is in place, the bits and pieces of the present curriculum—the history, humanities, language, the social and natural sciences, and all the rest—will be placed upon it. It will be shown that the traditional elements of the curriculum can be placed in a conceptual context that makes them a unified, coherent, logical whole—a curricular system.

The Key to Solutions

Improbable as it may seem, a single idea is the starting point for the construction of a dynamic, self-renewing, unified, conceptually integrated, reality-based, universal, and useful curriculum. Let me begin by identifying that idea.

Most of us bring to the learning process the same basic equipment: the physical senses. We see, hear, touch, taste, smell. That which we sense (if it is learned) is perceived, organized, and assigned value. The process begins as awareness begins. The image of a mother's face, the feel of a nipple, the sound of a creaking crib, the taste of applesauce, the smell of popcorn—all perceived, organized, and a value attached.

Although we all sense similarly, we do not perceive, organize, and value the sensed information similarly. Our approach to perception, organization, and valuation of sensed information is learned from those who rear us. Those who share a particular approach to perceiving, organizing, and valuing constitute a sociocultural system. There are a vast number of such systems on earth. Political boundaries sometimes, but not usually, coincide with the boundaries of sociocultural systems.

Each sociocultural system's way of perceiving, organizing, and valuing information gives it a view of reality unlike any other. This peculiar perspective permeates every thought, every statement, every action. We do not learn "what is", we learn what our native system's distinctive way of perceiving, organizing, and valuing allows or programs us to learn. In the attempt to understand reality, therefore (or the parts of it we call "history," "zoology," "humanities," "chemistry," or designate by other terms), the peculiar perspective or bias of one's native sociocultural system must be understood and taken into account.

Since the attempt to understand reality requires awareness of one's distinctive cultural perspective, and since awareness of one's cultural perspective requires an understanding of the cultural system which structured that perspective, a comprehensive study of anything must of necessity be accompanied by a study of its cultural context.

In our attempt to understand ourselves, each other, the earth, the universe—in our attempt to understand anything—the first and fundamental task is to determine the nature and limitations of our perspective. We look at reality not directly but through a "lens" created by our culture. That lens is ground to a prescription unlike any other. There are distortions in the glass. It is tinted a distinctive hue. Certain areas are cloudy, others opaque. Specks of dirt and dust adhere to the lens.

But never having viewed reality through any other lens, we assume that the dimensions of reality we perceive are accurate, that beyond the visible horizon nothing lies, that the shapes we discern are the actual shapes of reality. Unaware of our limited and biased perspective, we insist that what we see is all there is to see, that the science we practice is the only science, that the history we recall is the only history, that our approach to knowing is the only approach to knowing, that reality has only those dimensions which our measurements and our ways of measuring disclose. We fail to see that what we perceive is as much or more a product of the equipment we have created for viewing than of the characteristics of that which is viewed.

We do not really want to believe this. We find it difficult to accept that our own culture is not the one against which others should be measured. The cultural historian James Burke summarizes our assumptions:

> We have advanced from magic and ritual to reason and logic; from superstitious awe to instrumental confidence; from localized ignorance to generalized knowledge; from faith to science: from subsistence to comfort; from disease to health; from mysticism to materialism; from mechanistic determinism to optimistic uncertainty. We live in the best of all possible worlds at this latest stage in the ascent of man.

And then he identifies the foundation of our assumption of superiority:

> The generator of this accumulation of knowledge over the centuries, science, seems at first glance unique among mankind's activities. It is objective, making use of methods of investigation and proof that are impartial and exacting. Theories are constructed and then tested by experiment. If the results are repeatable and cannot be falsified in any way, they survive. If not, they are discarded. The rules are rigidly applied.

But Burke has led us into a trap. He summarizes our assumptions of the superiority of our view of reality, reiterates our conviction that our "science knows no contextual limitations, it merely seeks the truth," and then he says the following:

> But which truth? Different societies coexisting in the modern world have different structures of reality . . . [structures which] provide the user with hypotheses about events before they are experienced. The events then fit the hypothesis, or are rejected as being unrecognizable and without meaning. Without the structure, in other words, there can be no reality.

> In all cases of perception, from the most basic to the most sophisticated, the meaning of the experience is recognized by the observer according to a horizon of expectation within which the experience is expected to fall.

He concludes:

> The [culturally imposed] structure represents a comprehensive view of the entire environment within which all human activity takes place. It thus directs the efforts of science in every detail. In all areas of research, from the cosmic to the sub-atomic, the structure indicates the best means of solving the puzzles which are themselves designated by the structure as being in need of solution.

In *The Silent Language*, Edward T. Hall makes the same general point:

> There is no such thing as experience in the abstract, as a mode separate and
> distinct from culture. Culture is neither derived from experience nor held up
> to the mirror of experience. Moreover, it cannot be tested against some mystical
> thing thought of as experience. *Experience is something man projects upon*
> *the outside world as he gains it in its culturally determined form.*

And, from Donald T. Campbell:

> Hume taught us that scientific inference was logically unjustified. In the cur-
> rent generation the exciting intellectual developments in the philosohy of science
> represent rediscoveries of that truth in a much more specific and descriptive
> form. Science and ordinary knowing are now seen to be based upon deep-seated
> presumptions about the nature of the world. These presumptions, or others
> to take their place, are necessary prerequisites to perceiving and sciencing, but
> they are unconfirmable. In considerable part, these enculturated paradigms and
> presumptions will be specific to the culture of origin.

There is no escaping it. There are no earthly views of reality except through
cultural lenses. There is therefore no escaping the conclusion that what we ought
to be about *first* is the analysis of the particular lens that our native sociocultural
system has given us to use, and a comparison of that lens with those used by
other systems. No part of reality, no view of reality, no curriculum designed
to study reality, no discipline, no subject, no topic is objectively perceivable.
If we want to understand, we cannot merely study flowers, quadratic equations,
paranoia, and the Renaissance. We cannot know what they are until we know
who we are and how and why we see as we do.

The "distortions, the cloudy areas, the blind spots, the colors, the specks
of dust and dirt" are of course in our minds. They represent our inevitable
limitations when awareness is formed within the confines of a particular
sociocultural system. They begin to be apparent whenever there is interaction
between two systems, for the problems of perspective manifest themselves in
communication breakdowns, wasted motion, misunderstanding, frustration,
resorts to violence or apathy. Middle-class American officials design "nice"
housing for the poor. The poor destroy it. Irresponsible? Generally not. Two
different views of reality. The missionary's wife has "incurable" cancer. She,
patronizingly, allows the native healer to "lay on hands." The cancer disappears.
Coincidence? Two different views of reality. The general calls for air strikes to
destroy the villagers' will to resist. The villagers act as if nothing has happened.
Inscrutable? Two different views of reality. The visiting American explains that
practicing birth control will make possible "a better life" The proud father

of a dozen children is mystified by the American's strange definition of "better life." Ignorant? Two different views of reality. The Indian says he learned it from his grandfather, who was told it by the trees. The researcher suppresses a smile. Superstition? Two different views of reality.

Out of shared experience and speculation about that experience the members of each sociocultural system fashion a distinctive view of the world. And the world responds, assuring the members of each system that their particular version of reality is the right version—solid, enlightened, practical, indisputably and verifiably true.

Many of us feel that we have outgrown the peculiar viewpoint imposed by our own sociocultural system. Our education, our travel, our reading, and our perceptiveness have, we believe, made us conscious of and able to rise above cultural biases. It is not that easy. Even if we manage to identify and shed the unique perceptions of reality structured by our native culture, it is likely that we have simply exchanged them for the perceptions of another.

In every society, the study of the nature and implications of the shared view of reality is the foundation of the conception of humanness for those within that society. We can see the truth of this statement and appreciate the merit of it for others. We can see how revolutionary would be the effect if the misguided, the unenlightened, the prejudiced, and the superstitious would begin their education by examining the premises which confine, restrict, and structure their thinking. We have a great deal more difficulty realizing that our problem is the same as theirs and that we would benefit equally from such study. We view every topic, every subject, every discipline from a single, small, cultural platform. The position of that platform must be fixed for each of us before the observations we make from it can have their greatest meaning. Establishing the nature and location of that platform is the shared task which can integrate the curriculum.

It should probably be noted, parenthetically, that a discussion of cultural relativism encompasses ethical questions. On the matter of ethical relativism, I would say simply that it is sufficiently peripheral to the discussion to require no comment. Whether or not there are "better" or "worse" cultures or cultural value systems, whether or not there are transcendent truths or absolutes of goodness and beauty, whether or not individual teachers or insitutions choose to engage such questions are matters that lie beyond my present concern. I am saying only that every culture, including our own, comes to the task of understanding reality (and making judgements about the true, the beautiful, and the good) from an idiosyncratic position that must be taken into account, and that the major tool for taking cultural differences into account happens to be the most powerful device available for refining the general education curriculum. It would be unfortunate if an argument about ethical relativism diverted attention from this fact.

The case for making the study of sociocultural systems the core of the general education curriculum does not rest on a single argument. There are other powerful reasons for making such study the hub of the curriculum. One of these relates to perhaps the most widely agreed upon of all general education objectives—the necessity for understanding the self. The ancient injunction to "know thyself" simply cannot be realized independently of a comprehensive study of the sociocultural systems which structure the self's actions and thoughts. Every self is a part of a society composed of many such selves, all of which have been part of the same system since birth. From this system each individual has borrowed many ideas and ways of acting. In fact, nearly all the ideas and ways of acting we call our own have been acquired from our native society. The extent of this borrowing is not adequately appreciated, however, for the vast body of shared traits, like a familiar, steady noise, has disappeared from consciousness. What is noticed are the differences—the personality traits, the quirks, the individual idiosyncracies. These constitute only a relatively minor part of the total self, but they seem to be the whole of it, for the rest have slipped into the unnoticed realm of the too familiar.

To really know the self, all the vast *shared* ideas and patterns of action must be surfaced, must be moved from background to foreground, must become something of which the self is objectively aware. The familiar must be made strange enough to perceive, and that requires a comprehensive understanding of the sociocultural system of which one is a part. And, since awareness requires contrast, the characteristics of one's own sociocultural system are most clearly delineated when they are outlined against those of other, different systems. For those who believe that self-knowledge is an important objective of general education, the conclusion is therefore inescapable: sociocultural systems must be understood.

A third argument for the study of sociocultural systems stems from the deep-seated and widely shared human desire for alternatives, for choices, autonomy, and freedom. Given the opportunity, most humans seem to prefer to choose their own leaders, their places of residence, their clothes, their friends, their daily routine. In every society, patterns for each of these choices have been established, patterns which often allow some latitude for the choosing of alternatives. But the choices are limited. They are limited by what those within a system believe is acceptable. To a much greater degree, however, they are limited by an ignorance of alternatives. One cannot act or think in ways not known. To those with no conception of majority rule, for example, majority rule can neither be accepted nor rejected. There is no freedom to choose an unknown alternative.

Across the face of the earth there are countless patterns for living—patterns for work, play, organizing families, expressing feelings, being creative. Some of these patterns are potentially more valid, more useful, more appropriate, more satisfying than those we or others use, but they cannot be adopted because they are simply not known. The potential for freedom grows as options increase, and the most fruitful source of options is other sociocultural systems. Alternative designs for living can rarely be borrowed wholesale, but they are the richest of all sources of ideas. If we want access to freedom-expanding ideas, we must come to understand sociocultural systems.

To these reasons for making a study of sociocultural systems the formal core of the general education curriculum a fourth should be added. Since the traditional disciplines are (and unfortunately are likely to continue to be) the major vehicles for the presentation of content, those disciplines need to be broadened and deepened. Pushing the boundaries of one's discipline out to encompass the phenomena being studied as it is viewed by members of other societies often opens up new and exciting possibilities for study, provides fresh perspectives, and lessens the embarrassing tendency within some disciplines to overgeneralize.

Of course, not all those within the various disciplines agree that moving beyond the boundaries of their native culture would be stimulating or useful, or that it might add dimension to their discipline. Some reject the proposition that their field is in any important way affected by the perspective of the culture which created and sustains it. They believe that their discipline's methodology is too objective, its principles too demonstrably true to require any sort of "cultural color correction." Other fields of study may suffer from unexamined cultural biases, but in theirs, they insist, facts are facts.

Such ethnocentric positions are hard to counter because the culture which invented the discipline they believe to be culture free also invented the rules for establishing proof. As the passages from Burke quoted earlier indicate, if all the evidence which fails to support one's position is considered to be superstition or for some other reason is considered invalid, then of course one's own facts are the only facts. The definition of proof ensures it. One can help counter these kinds of ethnocentric tendencies by preceding or parelleling the study of a discipline with a study both of the culture which structures our perceptions of that discipline and of other systems which structure perceptions differently. This approach can also yield other unexpected and often delightful benefits.

To these four arguments for including a formal study of sociocultural systems in the curriculum another should be added. Sociocultural systems should be studied because they exist and because they are the basic units of human organization. Our preoccupation with and narrow conceptions of power cause us to focus much academic attention on presidents and prime ministers, reigns and regimes. But these are mere subsystems. Sociocultural systems are the entities that structure our daily lives. Scientific, systematic study is concerned primarily with the identification and analysis of patterns and regularities, and it is sociocultural systems, not political entities, which contain the most complete and coherent patterns and regularities. To know that a man is a Nigerian is to know very little about him. To know that he is Ibo or Hausa is to know a great deal. There are few if any Nigerian patterns of action and thought; there are enough Ibo and Hausa patterns to guide entire peoples through life for generation after generation. If we want to include human behavior on the list of phenomena to be studied in the systematic, organized manner of science, we must have integrated structures to study. Sociocultural systems are such structures.

Sixth, if there were no other reasons for studying sociocultural systems, the centrality of an understanding of them in our effort to exercise some control over our fates and futures would be reason enough. For nearly all the years of human existence, the quality of life hinged upon humankind's knowledge of the earth—the patterns of seasons, the habits of animals, the richness of the soil. But sometime not very long ago that ceased to be true. We have multiplied, crowded the land, organized nations, invented ways to talk over great distances, and move about with great speed. We have created vast, complex patterns which circle the earth and weave our destinies together.

Now, the intervals of time and space which once separated cause and effect, action and reaction have grown very short. Our margins for calculation of each other's intentions have become extremely narrow. The seasons and the soil still count, but for most of us the quality of life, and perhaps life itself, no longer depends upon our understanding of nature. It depends upon our understanding of each other. The understanding we need lies beyond mere common sense. It can only be acquired through a comprehensive, systematic study of sociocultural systems.

If the concept of sociocultural system is so central to the curriculum, if we maintain that it is the conceptual foundation of general education, that it ought to be so recognized and its potential formally developed, why was its centrality not recognized long ago? There are several possible reasons. One explanation is that we have not given the matter much thought, and when we come near to doing so, "common sense" interferes. We know we are human; know we belong to human society; know who else belongs to that society, what its boundaries are, and the nature of the rules and regulations delineating society's expectations. Common sense therefore suggests that all that it is really important to know about our society we already know. After all, have we not lived our entire life within it? Would it not be a waste to spend money and time teaching the young what they have but to live to learn?

The situation is not unlike that which Sir Isaac Newton might have faced if he had maintained to his neighbors that he had discovered the law of gravity. Would they not have insisted that they already knew about gravity, had in fact always known about it? It is unlikely that most of them would have immediately been able to appreciate the subtle but powerful difference between their pre-Newton "knowing" and their post-Newton "knowing what they knew."

The concept with which we are working—sociocultural system—shares with the concept of gravity the difficulties that arise from the proximity of that which the term represents. Discovery of the concept is even more recent than clarification of the concept of gravity in 1666, and for a great many reasons is considerably harder to conceptualize. It also shares with the concept of gravity the attendant difficulty that when the concept first begins to be understood, the phenomena it represents seem so familiar that it appears that nothing has been learned.

After its discovery, the concept of gravity assumed a central place in the thinking of everyone with an interest in physical phenomena. It became a given, *consciously taken into account* in every circumstance in which it might be a factor. Such has not been the case with the concept of culture. Although it is as central to the understanding of everything human as gravity is to everything physical, its centrality has not generally been understood and appreciated.

A second reason we do not appreciate the centrality of the concept of sociocultural system is that we believe we are already giving it the attention it deserves. We point to the fact that the nearly synonymous terms *society, social system,* and *a people* are part of casual conversation. We note that the terms are discussed in textbooks and classrooms and are referred to by all manner of individuals in all sorts of situations. The difficulty, however, is that our grasp of the concept would rarely qualify as understanding. It is as if our slight understanding of the concept of culture had inoculated us against feeling the necessity for real understanding. *Our assumptions notwithstanding, we do not teach the concept. It cannot be grasped as a single idea, and we offer students no systematic study of the myriad subconcepts and their relationships which collectively, and only collectively, give it meaning.*

In the attempt to understand human affairs, the concept of sociocultural system is not just another concept. It is *the* concept. When we really begin to understand it, we have no difficulty seeing why a grasp of it radically alters both our perceptions of the world in which we live and the courses of study we create to disclose that world to ourselves.

A third reason we have not recognized the centrality of the concept of sociocultural system is suggested by a review of scholarly effort over the last several decades. An attempt to see wholes, to get a view sufficiently broad to put components in perspective, is what generalists do. Unfortunately, there are hardly any generalists around, and the few there are command little respect. Even the scholars considered to have the broadest interests tend to be pre-occupied with what might be called "concepts of the middle range," with ideas such as scarcity, power, ecological balance, style, feedback. Those scholars with interests spanning all knowledge began to disappear, at least from higher education, decades ago.

The generalists are gone. They have been replaced not by specialists— not by linguists or economists or biologists—but by specialists within specialties, and even specialists within specialties within specialties. In fact, a review of academic programs would probably show that it is impossible to become a degreed generalist. There is no formal place in the academic world for those whose interests cross discipline boundaries. Within the disciplines, those with broad interests, according to prevailing views, should teach introductory courses. The "real" scholars—the specialists—should pursue research and sell consultant services. To many, the fact that it is often impossible or inappropriate to translate the generalists' interests into mathematical or computer models is proof of the insignificance of those interests. To the specialist, the generalist appears to serve little function, for the specialist's ability to see and evaluate the larger picture is seriously impaired by interest and training.

A fourth possible reason why we educators have not recognized the centrality of the concept of sociocultural system in our attempt to understand reality is our preoccupation with the arguments among the traditional contenders for attention. Caught up in the dialogue among those who think the curriculum should be based on the needs of students, those who think it should derive from the problems of society, and those who think it should rest on the content of the academic disciplines, it has not occurred to us that it might not be necessary to choose, that an approach could be devised which encompassed all three.

For these reasons, and very likely for others, the general education curriculum does not now include the comprehensive, systematic study of culture. It is hardly possible to overestimate the seriousness of the omission. Some of our students have not been taught to read, write, or compute well. We calculate the cost of that failure and are appalled. But almost none of our students have been taught to think about the fundamental nature and sources of human-ness. The cost of that failure—in lives lost, in resources forever gone, in wasted human potential, in richness of human relationships never realized—is incalculable.

A Solution

A coherent, integrated curriculum must be based on a coherent, integrated structure of meaning. Since meaning is based on culture, since the very same action, object, or observation can in two different cultures have two entirely different meanings, cultures are the largest, most complex, and most comprehensive entities in which all elements can be related systemically. Given our present level of understanding of reality, the concept of sociocultural system provides the broadest possible conceptually integrated base for the general education curriculum.

Sociocultural systems are complex, but they can be studied honestly and profitably by students of every age and ability level. The first step is to understand the role that models—simplified representations of reality—play in our thinking. Everything, even the simplest object, is too complex to be understood in a total sense. A dining room chair, for example, may seem ordinary enough, but from the standpoint of engineering design, component composition, or molecular structure it is very complex. If normal functioning required that we grasp or even consider this complexity every time we thought about chairs, we would be mentally overwhelmed. We are able to function because we create simple versions of things we think about and substitute those versions for reality. We think using models. A road map is a model—a simplified version of reality. So also is a recipe, a computer simulation, a chemical formula, a graph, a game of Monopoly, a medical diagnosis, a blueprint, a psychological profile. Everything we think about, we must model.

Models vary enormously in quality. A good model of spatial relationships in the solar system makes it possible to orbit Saturn with a spacecraft. Poor models of personality formation keep us from developing penal systems which decrease antisocial behavior. Good models of traffic flow allow traffic lights to be located and timed to minimize congestion. Poor models of the economy leave us uncertain about the cause and cure of inflation and depression. The final test of a model's quality is the accuracy with which it describes what will happen in reality. Good models will predict the flight characteristics of an aircraft still in the design stage, the reaction of a particular type of cancer cell to a proposed treatment, the response of a foreign government to a policy initiative. Good models answer all relevant questions, including those we neglect to ask.

Like chairs, aircraft, traffic flow, and the economy, sociocultural systems are things to be thought about. The quality of our models of such systems determines in large measure the quality of our lives—how accurately we interpret the past, how well we manage the present, and how precisely we predict the future.

Any number of models for representing sociocultural systems can be devised. In fact, most individuals already possess several. Whatever comes to mind at the mention of a particular people reflects one's model of that system, even if what comes to mind consists of nothing more than a mental image of certain kinds of facial features and characteristic modes of dress, a bit of information about the foods supposedly eaten, and a general idea of where the people live. A prejudice toward a particular society is a model—a simplified representation of reality. Stereotypes are models. *It is not a question of choosing or not choosing to use models to think about sociocultural systems. There is no alternative to their use. The only choice is between models of various quality.*

Obviously, models of sociocultural systems vary in their comprehensiveness, reliability, and usefulness. A model that includes only information about physical appearance or food eaten or area of the earth occupied is not likely to be of much help in predicting how the members of a system will react to the threat of invasion, an offer of assistance, the flooding of a river, or the discovery of vast oil reserves. Neither is such a model likely to explain very much about the structure of music or the shape of the living spaces which members of that system create, nor offer much insight into their assumptions about social responsibility or the functions of science or the role assigned to the supernatural.

A good model of a sociocultural system will provide a framework for description and analysis, identify relationships among various components, direct attention to causes and consequences of change, suggest potential sources of internal dissonance and external conflict, and point out long-term trends likely to have significant consequences. It will be a tool for explaining the past, understanding the present, and predicting the future. It will be a guide to the making of policy and a means for evaluating system health and stability or the lack of it. It will encompass every academic discipline. Finally, if the model is pedagogically sound, it will make all of this intellectually manageable by the average adolescent.

It is difficult to imagine any conceptual tool of greater value in the rethinking of the curriculum than a formal, comprehensive model for the study of sociocultural systems. Even for the most minor refining of traditional course offerings its usefulness should be apparent, for every component of the general education curriculum has the concept at its core. The most useful history and social science are concerned with the characteristics of, changes within, and relationships between sociocultural systems. The humanities are concerned with the imaginative productions of sociocultural systems. The earth sciences are concerned with the characteristics and conditions of the physical environments of sociocultural systems. Language is indissolubly linked to such systems—is in fact creator and the creation of them. And mathematics can have no greater challenge and no more worthwhile use than as a tool for tracing the shape of the present, the curves of history, and the probable and possible contours of the future of sociocultural systems.

As the core concept of sociocultural system is formalized, elaborated, and systematized, as it is made increasingly comprehensive and precise, all studies for which culture is the organizing concept will become increasingly comprehensive and precise. That is the thesis of this book. *'Sociocultural system' is the central pedagogical concept of general education. Teach it better and education will be better.*

In the chapters which follow, a comprehensive model for the study of sociocultural systems will be outlined. In its completed form, this model will do the following:

—Weld history, the social sciences, the humanities, the earth sciences, and the other components of the present general education curriculum into a unified whole

—Identify areas of study neglected in the present curriculum

—Make the components of the general education curriculum mutually supportive

—Establish criteria for determining the relative significance of subjects, topics, and concepts within the traditional disciplines

—Provide the curriculum with a self-renewing capacity

—Provide concrete, direct means for achieving the culturally approved, highest-level general education goals of American education

—Facilitate understanding and acceptance of relationship exploration, rather than information storage and recall, as the basic educational process

Before we begin the task of model building, here are several words of warning about possible difficulties of, and obstacles to, understanding.

First, it probably does not seem possible that the concept of sociocultural system could even begin to have sufficient depth or breadth to do all that I am claiming it can do. Adding to the possibility of difficulty is a widespread prejudice toward the social sciences. An approach to conceptual organization that seems oriented to the social sciences is, in itself, enough to trigger negative reaction in many scholars. For them, it may be difficult to suspend judgement sufficiently to give the concept an opportunity to demonstrate its power.

Second, some who until now have accepted the need for a formal study of culture may resist translating that rather vague and elastic concept into the concrete, specific instructional tool which a model represents. For them, the abstract terms *culture* or *a people* may have an appeal which the seemingly more mundane aspects of a model for study lack. As specific elements of a model begin to be identified and delineated, the educator may say, "Population density? I'm not interested in population density. What does population density have to do with music? With the weather? With political structure? With deviant behavior? With my interest in medieval religion?" To the scholar walking head down, eyes focused on a narrow, traditional path, any sort of relationship between, say, poetry and technology may seem too improbable or insignificant to merit attention. It may not be easy for specialists to stick with it, to believe that an exploration of that relationship could explain, enlighten, enrich, delight. Unable to see immediately how the seemingly alien is in fact integrally linked, they may leave the matter and never return.

Well, *is* population density related to anything else of importance? To self-concept? Yes. To patterns of family organization? Yes. To ideas about and attitudes toward nature? Yes. To technology? Yes. To music? Yes. To political structure? Yes. To . . .? Yes. A scholarly interest—any scholarly interest—which does not relate in significant ways to most aspects of sociocultural systems is probably not worth the scholar's time. Those who have little interest in what may seem to be the distant reaches of human societies—in demographic data, in the topography of a region, in patterns for distributing wealth or in ideas about the supernatural—may think these matters have little to do with each other or with those aspects of humanness in which they have an interest. They are wrong. Sociocultural systems are all of a piece. Everything of significance is related to everything else. Those relationships may not be immediately apparent, but they nevertheless exist, and no comprehensive grasp of humanness is possible unless the relationships are, if not exhaustively explored, at least appreciated. The scholar interested in architecture or government or philosophy who considers a discussion of weather, family organization, or weapons systems irrelevant has probably not pursued his or her interest very deeply.

A third possible difficulty: a model is, of necessity, a representation of reality constructed mostly of words. The familiarity and apparent simplicity of many of the words that will be used—*size, shape, time,* and *wealth,* for example—imply ease of understanding. However, not every reader may find understanding easy, for the words which appear in the model do not occur in the isolation they enjoy in the dictionary. Size as an abstract concept may, for example, be simple enough. But size as an element in a relationship, size as a characteristic of a society's environment affecting the behavior of its children or the design of its weapons or the relationship between neighbors within it complicates the intellectual task enormously. In systems, it is relationships which must be understood.

We usually underestimate the difficulty involved in grasping words, tend to assume that definitions teach, that dictionaries and glossaries explain. "Look up the definitions of these words," the teacher says, "learn the definitions, and use the words in a sentence." Acquiring understanding is not nearly that easy.

Our failure to appreciate how difficult it may be to learn a concept represented by a word stems mostly from the fact that, once we "know," we think the whole complex process of "coming to know" involved primarily the acquiring of a definition. If, for example, one has a good grasp of the mathematical concept of 'add', then the dictionary definition, "to combine numbers into a sum or total," seems to say something important and useful. But try a mathematical concept which may be less familiar: 'differentiate'. Does the dictionary definition, "to form the differential coefficient" provide a working grasp of the idea? If it does not, even looking up the definition of differential coefficient ("the limit of the ratio of the corresponding changes of function and argument, as the latter change approaches zero") may still leave one a little short of a working grasp of the idea.

We need a much greater appreciation of the inadequacies of our usual attempts to teach and learn using mere definitions. Despite its relative simplicity, a working grasp of the model I will be describing (or any other model for the study of sociocultural systems) probably cannot be acquired in a single reading. We must walk through new ideas slowly, measuring them against and illustrating them with our own experience. When that walk is taken with students, it may be necessary to stop often, or turn around and retrace steps again and again.

Yet another obstacle to the building of new conceptual models representing sociocultural systems is our old models of them. When, for example, we have grown up with a phrase such as "political, economic, and social" which categorizes human experience in one way, it is difficult to block it out and adopt alternatives.

The difficulties notwithstanding, in our attempt to grasp reality it is sociocultural systems we must come to understand. And how precise and extensive our understanding will be will depend upon the quality of our conceptual models. If we continue to ignore the need for formal models for the study of sociocultural systems, the conceptual tools our students build for thinking about them will remain unnoted, unexamined, unrefined, random, and disorganized. It is ironic that we presently help students create ever-more-elaborate and systematic mental models for thinking about technological systems, ecological systems, physiological systems, astrophysical systems, mathematical systems, and other kinds of systems, yet give them no guidance at all in the task of constructing conceptual models for the study of those most important systems of all—sociocultural systems.

An overview of a model for the study of human societies follows. It suggests that, in our attempt to better understand sociocultural systems, five kinds of information (illustrated by the following graphics) are especially useful:

1. Descriptions of the actual physical behavior of the members of the system — the patterns of action and interaction which structure daily activity

2. Identification and clarification of the major beliefs, assumptions, premises, and values held by the members of the system and underlying most action and interaction, particularly those shared ideas so taken for granted that they tend to be unstated and unexamined

3. Demographic data, primarily statistical, about the system's members — their number, age, and so forth

4. Information about the physical environment within which the system functions

5. Description and analysis of the relationships between these four — the system's patterned action, cognitive structure, demographics, and environment — with particular emphasis on the processes by means of which changes in various system components affect other components and the functioning of the total system

Neither the model described nor any particular model for the study of sociocultural systems is being promoted. A model is presented only to show that the single concept of sociocultural system, with an appropriate conceptual substructure, can indeed encompass, integrate, and organize general education and provide the other benefits claimed.

Notes

The Problems

That the present general education curriculum is unacceptable is so often noted in the literature and so obvious that it hardly seems necessary to provide additional documentation. A few observations beyond those already cited, however, may indicate the breadth of opinion supporting the contention that the general education curriculum is seriously flawed.

"The chaotic state of the baccalaureate curriculum may be the most urgent and troubling problem of higher education in the final years of the twentieth century." Mark Curtis, President, Association of American Colleges.

"[Science and mathematics] courses neglect the needs and interests of the vast majority of students... The present courses focus on pure science and are largely devoid of practical applications, technology, or the relevancy of science to society's problems." Karen Johnston, Professor of Physics, North Carolina State University; and Bill Aldridge, Executive Director of the National Science Teachers Association.

"Insofar as a true university should be responsive to major intellectual currents in the world, it must counteract the artificial fragmentation of knowledge enforced by the politics of hyperspecialization in the several disciplines." Gary E. Overfold, Associate Professor of Philosophy, Clark University.

"While a distribution formula may spread out a student's choices over a formidable array of courses, it is unlikely to provide coherence, integration, and synthesis. In fact, it is difficult not to be embarrassed by the way distribution requirements tend to reflect the distribution of departmental power, rather than a common and compelling vision of what should be taught and learned." Mervyn L. Cadwallader, University of Wisconsin.

"First, despite the staggering transformation in our understanding of biology and in our capacity to manipulate it, despite the technical, theoretical, and practical advances in the information sciences, we have not begun to incorporate the crucial area of science and technology into the liberal-arts experience that every student ought to have. We must fight the inappropriate fragmentation of the curriculum by disciplines." Leon Botstein, President, Bard College.

"The economists in their prescriptions and forecasts have been wrong so much in the last decade that one begins to wonder what the reason might be. The cause, it seems to me, might well be that their analyses lack the advantages of a multidisciplinary effort." Olaf Helmer, Rand Corporation, Inventor of the Delphi method.

"Our educational systems have modified themselves during the past 20 years, in response to internal and external pressures, so that they are now primarily designed to teach people specialized knowledge—to enable students to divide and dissect knowledge. At the heart of this pattern of teaching is a philosophical and epistemological view of the world that is quite simply false to the facts and realities as we now know them." James C. Coomer.

"The curriculum must be changed to multiply the links between mathematics and other disciplines." Lynn Arthur Steen, President, Mathematical Association of America.

"During the last few years, my concern about the state of the higher learning in America has reached the panic stage." Mortimer J. Adler, Chairman, Board of Editors, Encyclopaedia Britannica.

"Our report addresses the crisis in American education as it is revealed in the decay in the college course of study." "We do not believe that the road to a coherent undergraduate education can be constructed from a set of required subjects or academic disciplines." *The Findings and Recommendations of the Project on Redefining the Meaning and Purpose of Baccalaureate Degrees,* Association of American Colleges.

The Key to Solutions

Since making a conceptual structure for the study of sociocultural systems the basis of the general education curriculum appears to be a new idea, no scholarly opinion can be cited in direct support. There is, however, a vast body of work in several different fields from which support may be inferred.

At the most general level, the significance of our images of reality was early noted by Descartes and Galileo, who maintained that knowledge is neither more nor less than the power to manipulate the world according to the principles inherent in the particular model used to represent that world.

Botkin, Elmandjra, and Malitza, in their report to the Club of Rome titled *No Limits to Learning,* say the following:

> It is possible to read the history of humanity as a sustained effort to overcome complexity through increasingly refined and effective means first of representing reality and then of acting upon it . . . Today, the oldest sources of complexity, namely the universe and Nature, continue to pose a bewildering number and variety of facts and factors which astronomers and other scientists try to render intelligible by new theories and concepts . . . [but] there is another type of complexity of more immediate interest than that engendered by natural systems—a second-order complexity caused by human actions and man-made systems, and represented by a world of culture, civilization and human artifacts.

Broad support for conceptual model building comes also from the field of learning theory. Perhaps Jerome Bruner's *The Process of Education* deserves primary credit for raising the educational establishment's awareness of the role of cognitive structure in teaching and learning. An early quote from Ausubel provides a concise summary of the general view of most learning theorists about the role of conceptual structure:

> The principle of subsumption [classifying within a larger category] . . . provides a key to understanding the processes underlying the psychological accretion and organization of knowledge. The human nervous system as a data processing and storing mechanism is so constructed that new ideas and information can be meaningfully learned and retained only to the extent that more inclusive and appropriately relevant concepts are already available in cognitive structure to serve a subsuming role or to provide ideational anchorage. (Ausubel, *Education and the Structure of Knowledge*)

According to Bruner, the merit of a particular conceptual structure "depends upon its power for *simplifying information,* for *generating new propositions,* and for *increasing the manipulatability of a body of knowledge."* (Exactly. That is the criteria I would like applied to the conceptual structure I propose.)

The literature in the field is vast and accessible, and provides massive support for the proposition that understanding grows chiefly through a process of mentally organizing and unifying human experience. It would certainly seem to follow that a conceptual structure that helps organize and unify *all* experience is a move in the right direction.

Research bears out the fact that students perceive instruction that is formally and deliberately anchored in conceptual structure as superior. See, for example, the work of Janet G. Donald, Director, Centre for Teaching and Learning Services, McGill University.

From a very different body of thinking comes support for the adoption of a comprehensive conceptual structure. In a paper for a conference on science and culture sponsored by the American Academy of Arts and Sciences, Franklin L. Ford wrote the following:

> Culture properly defined for the purpose of educational questions implies the most ambitious and the most exacting intellectual effort and esthetic endeavor in every discipline. Thus defined, it also presupposes at least some exchange among the disciplines, some reciprocal curiosity and appreciation. In short, it necessarily involves a continuing tension between the centrifugal thrust of specialized exploration and a centripetal tug toward synthesis, toward the central area of shared concerns. What is worrying us now? Is it not precisely the suspicion that the centrifugal has triumphed over the centripetal, that the essential tension has disappeared—and with it, culture itself?
>
> As we contemplate this possibility, chilling in its implied finality, why do we tend so readily to focus our concern on the position of science? . . . Part of the answer seems to me to be that it is in discussing science that all who are concerned, scientist and non-scientist alike, see most clearly before them the threat that a synthesis of the human comprehension of the world may never again be possible, that culture as a thing shared may be lost forever to our species . . .
>
> Culture is always dependent and always will depend on how much that one knows can be explained to another.

Fundamental to understanding this chapter is the acquiring of what might be called an "anthropological viewpoint." The terminology may differ, but the importance of somehow getting "outside" immediate experience and acquiring a cultural perspective has been argued formally or is implicit in the work of many of history's respected scholars—Spencer, Taine, Comte, Mannheim, Tocqueville, Veblen, Durkheim, Weber—to name but a few.

In *The Sociological Imagination,* C. Wright Mills notes the kinds of questions the anthropological viewpoint encourages:

> 1. What is the structure of this society as a whole? What are its essential components, and how are they related to one another? How does it differ from other varieties of social order? Within it, what is the meaning of any particular feature for its continuance and its change?

> 2. Where does this society stand in human history? What are the mechanics by which it is changing? What is its place within and its meaning for the development of humanity as a whole? How does any particular feature we are examining affect, and how is it affected by, the historical period in which it moves? And this period—what are its essential features? How does it differ from other periods? What are its characteristic ways of history-making?

> 3. What varieties of men and women now prevail in this society and in this period? And what varieties are coming to prevail? In what ways are they selected and formed, liberated and repressed, made sensitive and blunted? What kinds of "human nature" are revealed in the conduct and character we observe in this society in this period? And what is the meaning for "human nature" of each and every feature of the society we are examining?

These are the kinds of questions the general education curriculum should prepare students to answer.

A Solution

As I have just noted, I am not advocating any particular model for the study of sociocultural systems. However, common sense and a considerable body of scholarly work support the validity of the general categories of the model I have identified.

Typical of the literature is this observation by Pitirim A. Sorokin: "Sociocultural phenomena have . . . a purely meaningful-ideological level, existing in the mind; a behavioral level, realized in the overt meaningful actions-reactions of interacting individuals; and a material level, objectified by and solidified into biophysical media of vehicles and conserves." Sorokin identifies three components, but two more are of course implicit in his comment. The individuals who compose the system are a fourth component, and the relationships among actors, ideas, action, and environment consitute a fifth.

Extensive, formal documentation of the validity of my five part model is not easy to find. In part the difficulty stems from the present emphasis on specialization and the general lack of interest in comprehensive models of reality. However, everyday experience affirms the validity of the categories. As we will see again later, drama and the novel are representations of reality which use the same five categories suggested here: (1) actors or characters [demographics], (2) stage or setting [environment], (3) plot [cultural premises], (4) action [patterns of action], and (5) drama or novel [systemic relationships]. My problem with documentation is about the same as would be encountered in an attempt to find a scholarly discussion of whether or not actors, stage, plot, and action were indeed proper categories for use in discussing drama.

Chapter 2

Organizing Knowledge

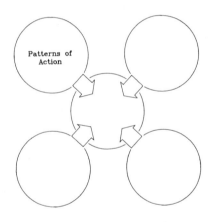

**Patterns
of
Action**

In a Bedouin camp, a child calls attention to a camel approaching in the distance. The men and children congregate in front of one of the tents to watch the arrival, while the women and older girls hurry away to the women's section. The man on the camel is identified as a Bedouin by his clothing—a red checkered headcloth held by a rope, a long white shirt, a dark brown cloak. Even at a distance, however, he is recognized as a stranger, for he wears his long hair braided and he rides sitting high on the center of the camel's hump rather than farther back as is the local custom. He approaches from the south, for that is the direction toward which the tents open, and even though the terrain is level, he pursues a slow, zigzag course, presenting first his left side to the observers, then his right.

To the Bedouin participants in this brief human encounter described by the anthropologist F.S. Vidal, there is very likely no awareness of the eight patterns just described. To them, a stranger has arrived in proper fashion. Even if they are familiar with patterns for arrival used by others, they are still not likely to stand "outside" themselves, look back in at the often-repeated ways of acting, and perceive them as patterns.

Nor do the members of any group find it easy to make the familiar strange and to see their own patterns clearly and objectively. Not only are those patterns too close to be apparent; they are hedged about with unexplored assumptions about what is right and proper and complicated by the symbolism attached to some of them.

Of the thousands of patterns routinely followed by the members of a society, relatively few are really important. Whether or not the members of a system eat with fingers or forks, drive on the left or the right, shake hands or bow when greeting makes little difference. The genuinely significant patterns are those which, if they change, reach out and alter other patterns of action, demographic characteristics, the environment, or the shared cultural assumptions of a particular sociocultural system. These kinds of regularities are the fabric of society. They are so fundamental that a slight change in any one of them will usually change all the rest. For example, a decision to invest in modes of production which call for a division of labor will have revolutionary, and generally unanticipated, consequences. The adoption of remote electronic shopping, the practice of isolating the elderly or actively integrating them into other patterns, the tendency of couples to marry at a particular age or to have families of certain sizes are other general patterns which ripple through a sociocultural system affecting much else.

In any attempt to understand a sociocultural system, the important patterns of action within that system must be noted. It is necessary to know who ordinarily does what, with whom, how frequently, for how long, where, with what—general questions, yes, but questions requiring precise answers if the nature of human experience is to be understood. Let us consider several patterns important in all sociocultural systems.

Socializing

In every society, the members have at least some free time, time when choices can be made about whom to be with and under what circumstances. The differences in patterns for associating vary enormously from group to group, and may also vary considerably over time within the same group.

A too-little-appreciated example of the latter can be found in relatively recent American history. For many Americans who are presently beyond middle age, patterns for associating during their early years frequently, perhaps almost always, put them in contact with others whose ages spanned from early infancy to old age. They attended small schools where ages may have ranged from five or six to the late teen years. In small rural churches they sat in congregations where infants in arms and the elderly were ordinarily in attendance. At social activities, suppers, games, work parties, and when hunting, for example, they shared the activity with participants of all ages.

The picture has changed radically. Rarely are children in school now closely associated with those whose ages differ more than a year or two from their own. Large religious organizations ordinarily segregate by age. Little League sports and dozens of other forms of recreation involve individuals of closely bracketed age groups. In less than a hundred years America has been transformed from a society in which most patterns for associating cut across all age groups to a society in which nearly all patterns for associating are rather narrowly circumscribed by age. No important aspect of American life has remained untouched by that change. Its implications and ramifications are vast.

In every sociocultural system, questions about who spends unstructured time with whom, doing what, when, where, and with what are of sufficient consequence to note. A model for the study of sociocultural systems should direct attention to shared patterns for socializing.

Working

Out of the driveway at 7:13 . . . wave goodbye to daughter, Cindy, still in upstairs bedroom getting ready for school . . . eight blocks, two stop signs and one traffic signal to outerbelt expressway ramp . . . six miles to north-south expressway ramp. 7:35 . . . one and a quarter miles to the off-ramp at 49th Street . . . bumper to bumper for the last seven blocks to the office . . . parking lot closed for paving . . .

One of the more intriguing aspects of computer technology is its potential for changing work patterns. For a few individuals, those changes have already begun. They work at computer consoles, and the consoles are in their homes. The product of their labor is converted to electrical pulses and transmitted elsewhere. "Elsewhere" may be across town, to a nearby city, or a point hundreds or thousands of miles away. "Going to work" means going into the bedroom or a corner of the kitchen. "The old 8 to 5" may be from 6 until 10, 2 until 4, or after the children have gone to bed. The car stays in the garage. The worker does not visit the office. There is no office, no executive restroom, no drinking fountain, no parking lot, no file cabinets, no Christmas party, no hierarchy of supervisors and managers, no company cafeteria.

All the world's work cannot, of course, be completed by computer. But a growing percentage of it can, and the number of individuals involved in that work is likely to grow very large, large enough to change traffic, change neighborhoods, change marital relationships, change parent-child relationships.

Changes in patterns for work nearly always have revolutionary consequences. Cottage industry, the use of animals, the factory system, division of
labor, the eight-hour day and forty-hour week, minimum wage laws, appren-
ticeship, mandatory retirement, child labor laws, the number of workers
required for a task, starting and stopping times, location—each pattern for
work has consequences and implications which reach out and structure ideas,
attitudes, and patterns for living. A model for the study of sociocultural systems
should direct attention to patterns for work.

Educating

In at least some Indian tribes, grandfathers once bore primary responsibility for teaching grandsons. The two of them might spend extended periods
away from camp following the trail of game, making tools and weapons,
trapping, coping with weather—the grandfather demonstrating, explaining,
testing; the grandson watching, listening, practicing. One can assume that,
generally speaking, it was a viable pattern for educating. Both teacher and
student realized the importance of the task and both probably found it
rewarding and fulfilling.

The arrangement for educating worked well because the grandfather knew
rather precisely what needed to be known. His survival was proof of that. He
knew the territory—the land, the animals, the elements, the enemies, the
problems, and the possibilities. Because the problems the grandson would
encounter would be more or less identical to those the grandfather had already
encountered, there was no doubt that what was being transmitted from one
generation to the next was valid and useful. The pattern for educating worked.

But eventually it stopped working, and the major reason illustrates why
patterns need to be identified, understood, and evaluated by those caught up
in them. The grandfather-knows-best pattern stopped working for most
American Indians when the knowledge needed for survival was not known by
the grandfathers. What many Indians eventually came to need was not primarily
an understanding of nature but an understanding of the intricacies of civil law.
They needed to know about treaties, contracts, mineral rights, severence taxes,
depletion allowances, and all the other provisions of the law which touched
on the holding, use, and management of Indian territory. Grandfather did not
have that information. Sometimes younger Indians did. At that point, a refusal
to change the traditional pattern for educating could become (and in many
cases actually was) the first step toward cultural destruction.

Educating is not a single pattern, of course, but a complex of patterns
having to do with who is taught what, by whom, where, how, when, with
what—a great many variables, but every one of them important. Left alone,

patterns for educating tend to become increasingly inappropriate. Eventually, the failure of sociocultural systems to evaluate their patterns for educating and to adapt them to changing circumstances may result in the disintegration of those systems. An exhaustive study of patterns for educating should be an integral part of every school's curriculum. A model for the study of sociocultural systems should include such study.

Controlling Behavior

Colin Turnbull, English anthropologist, lived for extended periods of time with the BaMbuti tribe of Pygmies in the Ituri Forest in Uganda. When the Pygmies made camp, he said, families constructed dwellings by bending green saplings to make a dome-shaped skeleton, weaving vines around the skeleton to make a latticework, and then covering the structure with mongongo leaves placed like tiles. Sometimes, Turnbull said, when a member of the tribe had behaved in a way the other members of the tribe considered objectionable, those living nearby would reorient the entrances to their dwellings so as to point away from the one occupied by the offender. When behavior was acceptable, entrances were returned to their original location.

This somewhat unusual pattern of behavior is but one of thousands devised by humans in the attempt to encourage adherence to approved patterns of action. Hester Prynne's scarlet letter was another approach. Gossip, ridicule, electrocution, banishment, ostracism, imprisonment, public hanging, excommunication, stretching on the rack, fingerprinting, derision, and fines also have that purpose. Sometimes rewards, prizes, bonuses, compliments, and promises are employed for the same reason.

Most members of most sociocultural systems adhere to most of the patterns of the systems to which they belong for reasons other than fear of the methods used to control deviance. Most often, of course, individuals do as they do because alternatives have not occurred to them or, if they have, the alternatives have little appeal. Adherence to patterns also frequently stems from beliefs about the expectations of others or of supernatural beings. Custom, habit, belief—whatever the first cause for adhering to prevailing patterns—the need to conform is communicated to the members of societies by a great variety of patterns.

The effectiveness of the patterns for controlling deviance are important, for if they do not work well, the system will tend to become unstable and may come apart. Each member must be able to predict with considerable accuracy how other members are going to act and react in every situation. It is necessary, for example, to believe that the drivers of oncoming automobiles are going to do everything in their power to stay in their traffic lane. The whole world functions primarily because people go where they are expected go, at approximately the expected time, and do what they are expected to do.

Patterns for controlling deviance can, however, work too well. In order to survive, sociocultural systems must constantly adapt to changing circumstances, a process that frequently requires replacing an old pattern with a new one. Since long-repeated patterns of action tend to take on an aura of sacredness, those who attempt new patterns are likely to be viewed negatively. If the techniques for controlling deviance are too effective, the resulting paralysis can result in the destruction of the system. History is full of examples, not often recognized, of patterns for controlling deviance so rigidly adhered to that necessary adaptation was impossible.

Tracing a path between instability and rigidity is one of the most complex challenges sociocultural systems face. Societies in which this problem is not understood are ill equipped to deal with it. A model for the study of sociocultural systems should direct attention to patterns for the control of deviance.

Distributing Wealth

In Thomas Jefferson's autobiography, he describes a project begun in 1777 to "create a system of laws" for the new state of Virginia. Jefferson was one of a committee of five appointed by the legislature and given responsibility for the task. He wrote as follows:

> I proposed to abolish the law of primogeniture, and to make real estate descendible in parcenary to the next of kin, as personal property now is, by the statute of distribution. Mr. Pendleton wished to preserve the right of primogeniture, but seeing at once that could not prevail, he proposed we should adopt the Hebrew principle, and give a double portion to the elder son. I observed, that if the eldest son could eat twice as much or do twice the work, it might be natural evidence of his right to a double portion; but being on a par in his powers and wants, with his brothers and sisters, he should be on a par also in the partition of the patrimony.

Jefferson and the four members of his committee understood and appreciated the importance of patterns for distributing wealth. They knew that acceptance of the principle of primogeniture would be followed by the creation of one sort of human society, and the rejection of the pattern would create another, very different society. If real estate passed intact from oldest son to oldest son, a permanent class of landed gentry would be created, and social, economic, and political power would tend to concentrate in their hands. If, on the other hand, all heirs were treated equally, wealth would tend to be in constant movement and would be more accessible to those of ability regardless of their order of birth. Equality of opportunity would be fostered. Jefferson once said he did not think it possible for a legislature to pass too many laws dividing up property.

All human systems develop powerful emotional attachments to their major patterns of action. To patterns for distributing wealth, this attachment is almost always particularly strong. Capitalism is a pattern for distributing wealth, and emotion about it often runs high. "From each according to his ability, to each according to his need" is a description of another pattern for distributing wealth. the pattern for distributing wealth called "feudalism" ordered much of the life of medieval Europe. Robin Hood's fame derived in part from his promotion of a particular pattern for redistributing wealth.

Large-scale patterns for distributing wealth are not the only ones of significance. In some societies, all family members, including grown children, pool their incomes. In others, each member of the family keeps possession and control of his or her own earnings. In some groups, alms giving and taking are of significance in the distribution of wealth. In others, the practice is almost unknown. The importance of the differences in cultural assumptions and premises which action patterns like these reflect and which the patterns help create could hardly be overestimated.

Patterns for distributing wealth are not, as Marx maintained, all-pervasive. They do not determine all other patterns. However, they probably do have a greater number of significant secondary influences on human affairs than any other pattern or complex of patterns. A model for the study of sociocultural systems should include a study of patterns for distributing and exchanging wealth.

Making Decisions

In the 1970s and 1980s, the American view of Japanese corporations went something like this: Japanese prices were lower because wages in Japan were lower. Their products were good because their plants and equipment were newer. They received all kinds of hidden support from the Japanese government, and they did not abide by the rules of fair trade.

To those who looked closely at reasons for the phenomenal success of the Japanese during this era, the explanations were inadequate. Far more important, most of them said, was the Japanese style of management. They pointed to American companies within the United States that had been taken over by the Japanese and then, with the same employees, the same wage scales, and the same plant and equipment, were able to markedly increase production, improve quality, and decrease employee turnover and absenteeism.

The heart of the Japanese approach to management was decision making by consensus. A very flat organizational structure was used, everyone involved in the organization communicated with everyone else, and nothing was done until everyone had an opportunity to contribute suggestions, understand the whole matter, and agree that a particular policy, procedure, or product was the most desirable. This approach contrasted with traditional American approaches to management, in which decisions were made at the top and imposed on those below.

The contrast in performance of corporations which practice consensus decision making and those which do not provides evidence that patterns for decision making in industry have far-reaching consequences. That the same proposition applies elsewhere—in politics, in education, in religious and civic organizations, in the military, in the family—should be apparent. This relevance stems in large part, no doubt, from the fact that in many societies the drive for some kind of personal autonomy is very strong. Most individuals seem to want to participate in the making of decisions which affect them, and therefore react negatively or positively to particular patterns for decision making depending upon the extent of their participation in the process.

It is interesting and sometimes helpful to know that in many sociocultural systems there is considerable consistency in all major patterns related to decision making. Authoritarian or participative patterns for making decisions in religious matters are often paralleled by acceptance of similar patterns in politics, education, industry, and the family. In other societies this consistency is absent and subtle psychological stresses often result. Middle-class American society exemplifies the latter.

Other Patterns

In addition to the patterns of action just identified, an overview of the important patterned action of any sociocultural system chosen for study ought to include several others. Patterns for ownership, for recruiting or replacing members, for play, for displaying status, for communicating, for social service, for defense, for special days, for worship, and for expressing creativity probably ought to be part of this study, as well as other patterns which may become apparent as a result of the observation of particular groups. In some societies, for example, patterns for manipulating the spirit world or nature through supernatural means are important.

In every case, however, shared patterns of action—the usual and typical ways the members of a sociocultural system behave—are a major source of insight into the nature of sociocultural systems and must be part of any model for their study. We will call this component of the model "patterns of action".

The following list includes most of the patterned activity within human societies.

— Making decisions
— Controlling behavior
— Educating
— Distributing / exchanging wealth
— Maintaining membership
— Maintaining the self
— Socializing
— Working
— Status

— Ownership
— Boundary control
— Communicating
— Esthetic expression
— Social service
— Mobility
— Special days, holidays
— Play
— Worship

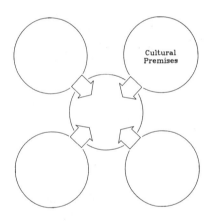

Cultural Premises

Every sociocultural system has a cognitive structure, a body of shared ideas, beliefs, assumptions, and values that differ from the structure of other socioculture systems. These states of mind are so deeply imbedded and so taken for granted that most of us are not conscious of them. If elements of their cognitive structure are pointed out to the members of a society, they will tend to think that, rather than being peculiar to their own group, the ideas are products of "human nature" and are shared by all "normal" human beings everywhere. The basic difficulty is suggested by the old saying "A fish would be the last to discover water."

One of several components of every society's cognitive structure is its time orientation. Middle-class Americans, for example, tend to be future oriented. They spend large amounts of time and money on education (and have a relatively low school drop-out rate) because they believe that sometime in the future this behavior will bring worthwhile benefits. They put money in savings accounts to buy future pleasure. They invest, confident that if they are patient the future will bring profits. They tend to live in a state of anticipation ("Just wait until I get my driver's license . . . a car of my own . . . an apartment . . . married . . . a house on Riverside Drive . . . a divorce . . . Just wait . . ."). The middle classes of other societies also tend to be future oriented, but most of the world's population is not. Some are present oriented, some past oriented, and others oriented toward life after death. To each society, the actions of other societies or subsocieties with different time orientations will either be incomprehensible or may seem unrealistic, irresponsible, or downright immoral.

Every society has a dozen or so fundamental premises which structure most of the actions of most of the members. What is considered the "best" time— past, present, future, or the hereafter—is only one. Assumptions about the nature of nature, beliefs about the causes of events and change, images of the good life, conceptions of the self, and ideas about the characteristics and role of the supernatural are others. Information about a society's premises is the most useful information that can be obtained about it, more important by far than facts about its economic system, its natural resources, its geography, its social structure, or its history. But premises are also inherently the most difficult of all instructional content, partly because, as we have noted, it is so difficult to take the first step—to realize that we ourselves have a distinctive way of looking at the world. We see the world not as it actually is but simply in the way the society into which we were socialized has taught us to look at it.

The members of a sociocultural system may not be aware of the premises which structure their lives, but those premises nevertheless are manifest in nearly everything they do. Within each system, the movements of dancers, the appearance and arrangement of buildings for work and worship, the holidays anticipated, the traits of heroes, the content of education, the shape of tools, the flow of musical compositions, the views from doors and windows—these and almost everything else of consequence will grow out of the shared premises of the members.

A dozen or a hundred eminent scholars from all parts of the world could be quoted to echo the late scientist and historian Carrol Quigley's statement that the cognitive system is "the most important thing we can know about any society."

The most important thing we can know about ourselves and each other and yet, incredibly, the study of cognitive systems is not in the traditional curriculum. It is not even being *discussed* by educators as a study which ought to be in the curriculum.

A comprehensive analysis of the many dimensions of each major cognitive system component is beyond the scope of this discussion, but a brief review of several should serve to emphasize their centrality to general education.

The Self

In the earlier discussion of patterns of action, it was noted that only a handful warrant detailed study. The same is true of the components of the cognitive system. Of the vast number of shared premises in every society, a relatively small number underlie nearly all significant behavior. These ideas tend to be those which grow out of what might be called "unavoidable aspects of experience." The surface of the earth, the objects upon it, the sky, people—these are aspects of experience so omnipresent that every society will have devised a body of ideas about them.

The self is one such unavoidable aspect of experience. Every individual is confronted by the fact of self—can look down and see the physical self or view its reflection in a pond or mirror. Around this fact of self the members of each society build a cluster of ideas. These ideas tend to be considered products of insight into the true nature of the self, but it would be more accurate to describe them as inventions or myths, products less of insight than of experience-triggered imagination.

Despite nearly-universal interest in the subject, the members of most sociocultural systems are not consciously aware of most of the ideas about the self they have acquired from their native system, ideas used constantly as guides to action, attitude, and feeling. One of those ideas, having to do with what might be called "boundaries of the self" as perceived by most middle-class Americans, can be inferred from the following. (1) The geographic distances between adult family members—between grown brothers, sisters, and parents—is often too great to permit frequent family get-togethers. Not infrequently members do not even live in the same state. This is not considered unusual or particularly undesirable, and no great effort is made to move family members closer together. (2) The incomes of adult family members ordinarily vary, sometimes greatly. This disparity is generally accepted, does not lead to feelings of guilt or anger, and is not considered unfair or inequitable. (3) In most instances, it is usual to contract with a corporation to provide assistance in time of need. Insurance can be obtained to replace lost income in case of illness or accident, to pay for hospital or nursing care, to replace lost or stolen goods, to cover costs accompanying death, or to assist in other emergency situations.

The members of many sociocultural systems would consider these American practices not only strange but unacceptable. To be cut off from one's family or clan for long periods of time would, they feel, deprive one of one's principal source of happiness—would, in fact, make life hardly worth living. Neither could any honorable reason be advanced to explain why members of the very same family would choose not to share incomes so that each could live as well as the others. And finally, to go to strangers if one were ill or in need of money would be unthinkable—an affront to one's family and threat to an arrangement which provides dependable, concerned care.

Two differing conceptions of the nature of the self help explain these very different practices. A metaphor may clarify: individual Americans tend to be "marbles"; individuals in some other societies are "fingers on a hand." Marbles may be held together, but even when they are squeezed tightly in a "family," they remain separate, distinct. Size, color, and configuration (identity) remain unchanged by the closeness. And if the hand is opened, the marbles roll off in different directions, still unchanged.

But fingers are different. If one is a "finger" one is an organic part of something else, something larger and more important. There is a sense of distinctiveness (no two fingers are alike) but not of separateness. One functions most effectively in concert with others, in fact *can* only function effectively *with* the rest of the family. The welfare of each is bound up in the welfare of the whole. To be cut off, to have no close, working relationship with the family, deprives one of the most fundamental reason for existence. One might as well be dead and, in a few groups, death appears to actually result from separation. The individual continues to eat, continues to drink, continues to maintain physical care of the body, but dies nevertheless.

A discussion of the self as marble or finger barely begins an exploration of the concept. In some societies, conceptions of the self seem inextricably linked to dead ancestors and unborn descendants—in others, to the political state. In some, the use of phrases such as *a child of God* or *at one with the Spirit* suggest still other perceptions of the boundaries of the self.

Different answers to the question, What are the boundaries of the self? help explain differences in behavior from society to society. Other questions related to individual selves are equally important. Are individuals within the system of equal or of varying worth? Is perceived worth a constant, bestowed at birth and continuing in full until death, or does it vary with age, sex, birth order, family? Is the self inherently good, inherently bad, or "neutral"? What are the rhythms, stages, cycles, or states of the self? What is its structure? (For example, Americans tend toward a fragmented conception of the self, the self as several selves—physical, mental, emotional, spiritual.)

In every sociocultural system a range of ideas having to do with the nature and identity of the self have evolved and are shared. These ideas give a distinctive character to the economic, political, social, esthetic, and religious activity within the system and should be identified and studied.

Significant Others

"Sixty-Three Killed in Plane Crash," says the newspaper headline. The reader brings the paper closer. Eyes move from line to line down the page. When the sentence "No Americans were reported aboard" is reached, many Americans move to a different news item.

All humans look out from the vantage point of the self and see other human beings. For any number of reasons, including dependency, proximity, instruction, and experience, these others tend to be viewed as having varying degrees of significance. If one visualizes a series of concentric circles with the self (usually, but not always) occupying the innermost circle, significant others are those who occupy the other circles, their relative significance represented by their distance from the self. How much of the news story is read depends largely upon the positions of others on this circle. If reading stops when identity has been established, one must assume that those who were killed are not particularly significant to the reader. Indeed, the very fact that some version of the sentence appears at all suggests that, to the writer as well as the reader, the world is divided into individuals and peoples of varying significance.

The criteria for ranking others according to degree of significance are often affection, honor, or respect. Perhaps the most useful approach to identifying shared assumptions about relative significance is to rank others on the basis of the amount of activity attributable to a relationship and the intensity of feeling which accompanies the activity. For example, for most Americans, neighbors were once very significant others. This is hardly the case today.

Every individual's significant others will of course differ, but in every society certain tendencies will be apparent. In some, parents will rank next to or even above the self. In other systems, religious leaders will be very significant. Grandparents and other family members will be considered more or less significant depending upon the group. Sometimes even rather distant relatives will rank above friends. In some groups, workmates are particularly significant. In others, they count for little unless they are also friends.

The concentric circles can be usefully extended to include large categories of people. Nationalities, races, ethnic groups, or those with certain religious affiliations, for example, can be ranked according to degree of perceived significance. Because each category of significant other carries with it expectations, obligations, responsibilities, and attitudes which result in modes of behavior, making sense of the patterns of action within a sociocultural system requires an awareness of who counts for how much.

Causation

The sun comes up. The baby gets sick. A war breaks out. Flowers bloom. A lost key is found. It rains. The cathedral catches fire. A bus skids on the wet pavement. A tiger attacks at the watering hole. The cancer disappears. The potatoes rot in the ground. Money comes unexpectedly in the mail. The volcano erupts. The snow is dry. The leak stops.

Why? No one knows for certain, but the members of every society believe they know, believe they can explain, at least in general terms, the causes of most consequences. They also believe that the explanations they advance are so obviously true, so logical, so objectively verifiable, so far beyond question, that discussion of them is almost pointless. Further, they believe that other explanations of why things happen are so absurd, so illogical, so demonstrably false that they could only be a product of naivete, superstition, ignorance, or perversity.

Why does it rain? It rains because atmospheric conditions are conducive to rain. It rains because, in the Grand Design, each rain is preordained. It rains because, through the rain, God can manipulate the beliefs and attitudes of humans. It rains because the rain ritual has been performed so precisely that there is no alternative to rain. It rains because the Spirit of the Rain wishes it. It rains in response to faith. There are dozens, perhaps hundreds of "reasons" why it rains. In every group, one or two explanations are believed implicitly. The rest will not be considered of sufficient merit to be taken seriously.

Why does the stomach ache? It aches because of a chemical imbalance. It aches because the mouth was open in the presence of those who cause evil spirits to enter. It aches in order to punish. It aches because a pin has been inserted in a voodoo doll. It aches because Fate wills it . . .

A considerable variety of assumptions about causation are held by groups within the United States. The dominant society tends to put great store in two principal explanations: (1) things happen because of the operation of chemical and physical forces, and (2) things happen because humans make them happen. The operation of chemical and physical forces explains rain, volcanic eruptions, stomach aches, television, sunsets, and hardening of the arteries. People are responsible for wars, traffic accidents, fund drives, hospitals, concerts, murder, taxes, and poverty.

School textbooks teach these two "primary causes," the media reinforce their centrality, and common sense and science are cited in support of their validity. Effects which are different or impossible to trace to one of these causes are generally ignored or attributed to trickery. Those who show interest in other possible causes are viewed with suspicion and, if the interested party is engaged in research, funds are usually very hard to obtain.

Space

Sociocultural systems exist in physical space. Over long periods of time, various attitudes and assumptions about this space evolve and begin to structure action. As with all components of a society's cognitive system, however, neither the distinctiveness of these ideas nor their implications are ordinarily recognized by those who share them.

One of the more familiar illustrations of this fact has to do with the idea of personal space—the "bubble" extending outward from the surface of the body that is felt to be one's private domain. It is surprising how few individuals have attempted to trace the outlines of their own personal space or have given thought to variations in it related to particular others. Nor are many aware of differences from group to group in the size and shape of personal space and the reactions to various kinds of perceived violations of it.

Personal space is but one space-related component of a society's cognitive system, and perhaps not an important one. It can be a source of irritation and misunderstanding, and it may occasionally contribute to small-scale problems, but the fact that a group's ideas about the proper dimensions of personal space can apparently change without altering other premises or patterns suggests that it is usually not very significant.

Other space-related concepts, however, have behavioral consequences. Traditionally, Bolivian tin miners show respect for "Tio" when they go underground, for they believe that Satan is preeminent in the space below ground level as Christ is preeminent in the space above. Between the Army Corps of Engineers and various Indian tribes there is a long history of conflict traceable to differing assumptions about certain spaces. In ancient Israel, that portion of the temple called the "Holy of Holies" was related to differently than other space. Sacred groves, burial grounds, altars, haunted houses, and the locations of supernatural manifestations or important historical events are also often treated differently, and almost always require changes in behavior when one is at or near them. Even feelings about the relative desirability of residing in the bush, on the mountain, at the seashore, or "beyond the sound of another man's axe" are space-related ideas that help explain patterns of human behavior.

Ownership

It is Christmas morning before dawn. The children, just awake, run down the steps and into the living room. Unopened packages pyramid under the tree and spill out across the carpet. Catching the light is a new bicycle. A tag hangs from the handlebars. "Merry Christmas," it says, "from Mom and Dad to the Children."

It is not difficult to imagine the consequences of such a gift. American children, like their parents, tend to assign ownership of the various parts of the material world to individuals and are ill prepared for most alternatives. Bicycles, and just about everything else, are supposed to belong to some*one*.

From the assumption that bicycles, automobiles, houses, farmland, forests, mountains, and minerals (and decisions about their use) should be in the hands of individuals, much follows. From the assumption that much or all is owned jointly by all members of a society, much of a very different nature follows. From the belief that entities call "corporations" can be created which, like individuals, can own and control but, unlike individuals, need never die, yet another cluster of effects follows.

The answer to questions about ownership have much to do with how life is lived. Who can own? (Males? Children? Spirits? Those of a particular religious affiliation?) What kinds of things can be owned? (Personal effects only? Land? Water? Symbols? Other humans?) How extensive are the rights and privileges which accompany ownership? (Can one do anything one wishes with that which is owned, including destroy it? Is ownership transferable? Is it held in trust?) What special responsibilities does owning entail? What obligations, if any, accompany ownership?

Beliefs and assumptions about ownership send out tentacles which reach into the remotest parts of sociocultural systems, affecting how individuals act, how family members relate, and how institutions and nations function.

The Good Life

The members of every sociocultural system share some kind of mental image of the most desirable style of life. This mental image of "the good life" helps explain much human action—everything from the kind of education parents fashion for their children to the nature of the most common kinds of criminal activity. In evaluating an educational system, most parents really want to know if it will enable their children not so much to be educated as to achieve the good life. The criminal is striving toward the same objective, but using a different strategy.

Concern for the good life manifests itself in innumerable ways. The 1920s political slogan *two chickens in every pot* presented an image of the good life. The heading *Be Your Own Boss* in boldface type in the classified section of the newspaper is an attempt to use perceptions of the good life to attract attention. The advertising photographer who fills his backgrounds with out-of-focus but descernable symbols of the good life is attempting to associate the product being promoted with achievement of the good life, even if the two are logically unrelated.

"The Good Life" as a title for a general cognitive system category provides a rather large umbrella for several ideas which provide insight into the nature of human societies. Although "good life" ideas tend to be more concrete and more recognizable to members than other cognitive system elements, there is nevertheless a tendency within all groups to feel that one's own conceptions of what constitutes the good life reflect basic human nature and are therefore shared by the members of all other groups. To the American, it is easy to come to the mistaken conclusion that the desire for upward mobility goes along with being human. It may be hard to imagine, for example, that a situation in which mobility is possible and encouraged could be seen as threatening. For much of the world's population, however, that has been and is the case. More concerned about the possibility of downward movement than attracted by the possibility of climbing, the members of many societies have preferred rigid arrangements which guarantee position even if that position is low.

Since most conceptions of the good life are easily translated to value terms, one of the most direct ways to summarize a group's image of the good life is with statements such as *It's good to move up* or *It's good to know one's place.* Here are several additional statements drawn from various societies that reflect their conceptions of certain elements of the good life:

It's good to be young, beautiful, and active.

It's good to have many male children.

It's good to own lots of things.

It's good to be old and respected.

It's good to win.

It's good to avoid satisfying physiological desires.

It's good to be dependent.

It's good to hide one's true feelings.

It's good to be indistinguishable from others.

It's good to be clean.

It's good to be part of a network bound together by obligations.

Because ideas about the good life are usually the most familiar component of a group's cognitive system, they are sometimes questioned or subjected to rational analysis. When that happens, individuals may attempt to reject one or more of the group's shared conceptions of the good life. However, the power of early socialization is such that this is not easy to do. What often happens is that the individual will indeed alter certain behavior related to the rejected value, but will fail to see that other behavior continues to reflect the old value. For example, the middle-class American may label as shallow the accumulating of material goods yet continue to be impressed by those who have in fact acquired much.

Those who have not become objectively aware of their society's conception of the good life are prisoners of that conception, for they cannot choose to accept or reject ideas for which there appear to be no alternatives. Common sense and everyday experience do not provide either a clear picture of one's own images of the good life nor of possible alternatives to that image. A systematic study of the matter belongs in the curriculum.

Other Shared States of Mind

In addition to those cognitive system components just identified, all societies hold other important premises, including ideas about the nature of nature, about other societies, about trends and directions of change, about their own patterns and premises, about the meaning of existence, and about the supernatural. And, as was noted earlier, assumptions about and orientation to time also lie near the center of human behavior. Some societies (but perhaps not middle-class Americans) have very important premises about the individual's responsibilities to the society as a whole.

No truly satisfactory category system for cognitive system analysis has as yet been devised. The categories used here are not discrete, the same information could be categorized in a variety of ways, and important cognitive dimensions have no doubt been overlooked. But a start must be made and crude tools are better than none. Nothing that humans can know about themselves is more important. Sociocultural systems must be understood, and to understand them the cognitive orientations which give each of them a distinctive configuration must be studied. "Studied" does not mean that cognitive structures are made the focus of a two-week instructional unit or a one-semester course. It means that year after year, in subject after subject, what is taught is deliberately related to the fundamental states of mind which give human societies their form and determine their direction.

Cultural premises provide the content for the second major component of our model for the study of sociocultural systems. Most of the assumptions, beliefs and values underlying human behavior fit within one or more of the following categories:

— Self
— Significant others
— Nature
— Time
— Space
— The Supernatural
— Causation
— The "good life"
— Trends
— Acceptable / unacceptable action
— Meaning / purpose of existence

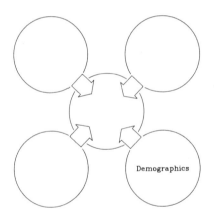

Demographics

The level of abstractness of cultural premises and patterns of action and the difficulties involved in perceiving them may initially make these two kinds of information about a sociocultural system rather hard to grasp. The kind of data subsumed under the title *demographics* creates no such problems. It is simple, direct information of the sort usually acquired in censuses, and can be presented easily in statistical or graphic form.

Number

Sociocultural systems are of course composed of individual human beings. From the number of these individuals much else follows. Schools with fifty students will differ in myriad and fundamental ways from schools with five hundred and five thousand students. The same will be true of corporations, tribes, neighborhoods, and nations. The size of membership will affect every major aspect of a system's internal dynamics and external relationships.

Establishing the number of members in a system may be easy—perhaps as simple as counting all individuals wearing a particular uniform or residing in an isolated valley. However, deciding who does and who does not belong to a particular system is often rather difficult. Race, color, and place of residence or occupation do not establish membership. What counts are shared patterns of action and state of mind. Counting is also complicated by the fact that several different sociocultural systems often occupy the same general area and share many patterns of action and meaning. Boundaries can be very fuzzy. Just what is designated a system also depends in part upon the objectives of study. A sociocultural system could conceivable range from a couple to a civilization, although entities such as French Canadians, Samoans, middle-class Americans, and Tibetans would be more typical.

Age

How many hospital rooms or outboard motors are going to be needed in seven years? What tendencies in the crime rate can be expected? How many contributors to the social security system will there be in the next generation? Are more or fewer doctors going to be required? In what direction is the general political orientation of the country likely to evolve? What will happen to the Cadillac division of General Motors if Cadillac's image does not change?

Information about the relative number of individuals in various age groups can help answer an enormous range of questions. In all sociocultural systems, each age group has a variety of tendencies, characteristics, responsibilities, interests, roles, and problems which translate into patterns of action. One age group will be unproductive and dependent. Another will be involved in instruction for adulthood. Others will be consumers of certain kinds of goods or services—will be in need of dwelling space, work animals, insurance, tools, or "the latest hit single" Others will be expected to fight, to give a period of time to public service, to fulfill some religious responsibility, or to bear children.

Because the actions of each age group place certain demands on the whole, create peculiar problems, drain certain resources, require special facilities, expand certain capabilities, or limit potential, information about the actual and relative size of age subgroups or those in various life stages is essential. Information about the size of age groups approaching different life stages is also of great value.

Sex

Members of societies in which the ratio between females and males has long remained unchanged are likely to have little awareness of the extent that actions and ideas are geared to the prevailing ratio. It is only when a long-prevailing ratio changes, or when another society with a differing ratio is studied, that the far-reaching ramifications of the relative number of each sex become apparent.

If nature were the only operative factor and the balance between the number of male and female births were always relatively constant, there might be less reason to include information about that ratio on the model. But balance is by no means ensured. War is a major creator of sexual imbalance in many groups. In others, the pursuit of a livelihood, the search for adventure, or adherence to a religious precept may create major or minor differences in the number of participating males and females. There is also the possibility that in the future technology might permit parents to select the sex of the desired child, with resultant social ramifications.

Whatever the situation—balanced, unbalanced, static, or changing—the sexual ratio within a sociocultural system has such an impact, and affects in such myriad ways other elements of the system, that prevailing and potential ratios must be known and their implications understood.

Distribution

To the traveler rounding a bend in a rural road in Europe, a dozen or so buildings will often appear, closely packed, houses and sheds almost leaning against each other. The road may narrow, zig-zag between the buildings, then open up once more to a countryside with no structure visible anywhere. Along the highways of Indiana, Illinois, and much of the rest of rural America, the scene is different. Isolated houses stand in the centers of farms or sit alone by the road, often far beyond convenient walking distance to the next house.

The difference is important. In myriad, subtle ways, patterns of action and interaction and the attitudes and feelings which accompany those actions are in part a product of the distribution and density of the population. Is it clustered in groups? Concentrated in a single, compact area? Ranged along the banks of a river or the edge of a forest? Shelved on the levels of high-rise structures or ringing an oasis?

Density and distribution of population do not determine life style or institutions, but they exert considerable influence toward certain kinds of interactions and make other kinds of interaction very difficult. It would not be likely that the population of an area in rural Idaho could assemble a symphony orchestra, or that the residents of Manhattan could organize to provide their own food supply. Ways of relating, organizing for action, dividing work and responsibility, controlling deviance, expressing creativity, educating the young—most collective and individual effort is shaped in part by the number of others involved and their physical distance from each other.

Information about the number, age, sex, distribution, density, and inherent physical or mental capacities and capabilities of those who together constitute a sociocultural system is the third major component of our model. I will call this component "demographics". Major categories of demographic data are listed below:

— Number
— Age
— Sex
— Capacities / capabilities
— Distribution
— Density

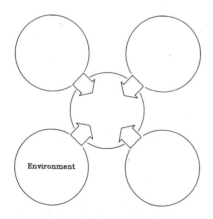

Environment

Imagine a vast shopping mall, open for business, colored lights playing on a central fountain, neon signs flashing, merchandise stacked on shelves and racks, climate control system maintaining temperature and humidity, cash registers and computers turned on and warm—and not a human anywhere. Move outside into a warm summer evening, to a parking lot filled with empty automobiles, then beyond to streets where more empty cars sit with engines running. Traffic signals change but no cars move. Telephones function, but no one calls. Television screens display test patterns or taped images, but their are no viewers. Out on the edge of the city, empty airplanes sit on lighted runways, radar antennas rotate but no one interprets the data. Diesel locomotives attached to strings of freight, tank and passenger cars stand in switchyards with engines idling, but there is no human presence.

These are the elements of an environment, the urban American's environment. It is a stage with props, a space with equipment, a setting, a place where a human group pursues its patterns of life. Every society occupies space, and the nature of that space—its size, shape, climate, resources, and the tools and other accumulated paraphernalia of the past which fill it—bend, mold, and stamp those within the space, organizing their lives, defining their problems, shaping their creativity, limiting their dreams.

Constructions

Houses used to have attics. The residue of generations accumulated there, and on rainy days children could spend hours with objects and items belonging to parents, grandparents, and other family members. Clothes, scrapbooks, toys, photographs, and much else could be looked at, tried on, played with, studied.

Most newer houses do not have attics. They add to construction costs. Roofs are now supported by low, light-weight trusses which make the use of attic space difficult and impractical. The objects and items which might once have found their way to the attic are now usually discarded—given away, set out to be picked up by the trash collector, or saved for a time and then sold at a garage sale.

Does such a minor change in the shape of the environment make any difference? It may. The difference may be subtle, but surely it exists. The child who spends long afternoons carefully scrutinizing and touching evidence that his or her parents were once also small, that they played with toys, wrote in childish scrawls, won trophies, valued certain useless things—surely that child is different, albeit in some indefinable way, from the child whose environment testifies that only the present is tangible and valued.

The houses and neighborhoods of eighty or so years ago and those of the present differ in other ways. The glass in the front door, once constituting most of its area, has shrunk to the size of a tiny button or has been entirely eliminated. The front porch is gone, and with it the porch furniture. The clothesline has been replaced by a dryer. The alley is no longer considered an economical use of space and developers leave it out. Heating and cooling systems create steady background noises which blot out the sounds of the neighborhood. Garages are attached, and remote-controlled doors make it possible to leave the neighborhood with a minimum of human contact. There are fewer vacant lots, fewer paths to isolation, fewer places of natural danger. The shape of the environment has changed, and every change has made a difference in how people relate to the world, to each other, and to themselves.

It is not just the shape of neighborhoods which affects the nature of human experience. Tenth-grade world history textbooks teach that the history of ancient Greece was in part a product of the rugged terrain of the Greek peninsula. Appalachia was for long a distinctive cultural region because of its relative inaccessibility. Research indicates that ceiling height, wall color, and other physical features of a room directly affect conversation and other behavior. Longtime operators of bars and restaurants know that seating arrangement, booth style, restroom location, and many other design features affect in important ways the length of customer stay, the likelihood of violence, and the money spent.

Millions of dollars have been invested in studies to design supermarkets which manipulate shoppers. Hundreds of department stores have gone to great expense to relocate escalators less conveniently so as to increase customer exposure to "impulse items." Jane Jacobs and others have shown that length of city block, street, and parking lot dimensions, building height, classroom arrangement, and just about every other feature of the physical environment contribute in powerful ways not just to action but to feeling and thought.

This is not an esoteric, marginally important subject. The shape of the environment has an enormous impact on family relationships, spending patterns, neighboring networks, crime and violence, educational effectiveness, business success, and almost every other aspect of daily life. One would suppose that a study of the relationships between human activity and the shape of created structures would be an academic discipline and an integral part of the general education curriculum. It is rarely even mentioned.

Resources

The young Asian girls stands facing a sun-warmed brick wall not far from the commercial heart of the city. She stoops, acquires a large handful of dung from a bucket, and plasters it neatly on the wall to dry. The geometric pattern she has created spans from sidewalk to as far as she can reach and back to her left to where the wall turns a corner. A small boy brings another container and the pattern lengthens. The dried cakes of dung will fuel family fires for cooking and for night-time warmth.

'Resources' can be an unwieldy concept. One group's pollution can be the mainstay of another group's economy. One era's resource base lies, in another era, unused and unwanted. That which has no apparent value can become, because of technological changes, almost invaluable. The resource picture can be relatively simple, as it is for those groups that require little more than grazing land and water. Or it can be complex, with resource needs encompassing most of the known minerals and energy sources.

Almost every elementary school child has studied resources extensively, and may be able to name the major ones upon which the economies of several nations depend. But a simple cataloging of resources is of little benefit in the attempt to understand the functioning of sociocultural systems. It is relationships which matter, relationships between a people's resources and their states of mind, relationships between their resources and their patterns of action, relationships between their resources and their demographic characteristics. Some of those relationships are so direct and obvious that there is hardly room for discussion. Others however are not at all apparent. Those are the ones to which a model should call attention.

As the world begins to face the hard facts of increasing scarcity, students, and the rest of us, need conceptual tools for anticipating and coping with the society-shattering potential. A model can provide many of those tools.

Climate

In 1915, Ellsworth Huntington wrote that the rise and fall of civilizations follow a six-hundred-year cycle. He believed that when global changes in climate blessed for a time a particular region of the earth, productivity and power for the people of that region followed. It is, of course, not that simple, but there is no denying that changes in climate relate to changes in human affairs.

The first great civilizations of Sumeria and Egypt formed during a period beginning about eight thousand years ago known as the Climatic Optimum. The later trends in climate which changed the Fertile Crescent to desert were surely a factor in the demise of those civilizations. It was very likely a period of cooling that, beginning about 2,000 B.C., pushed Hittites, Medes, Aryans, and Dorians south as invaders. Later, climate cooperated as Greece and Rome rose to power. The southward movement of Germanic tribes that overthrew Rome coincided with increasing harshness of climate in northern Europe.

Propitious climate brought prosperous, food-producing colonies to Greenland and Newfoundland, and the advancing cold of the Little Ice Age appears to have destroyed them. That era ended about 1875, and from then until 1940, in the northern hemisphere, the warmest weather in the last four thousand years prevailed. During that time industrialization peaked, the population more than doubled, and American food production expanded again and again.

The individual is aware of immediate climate conditions and perhaps of relatively short-term trends over a few years. However, unaided memory is too short and the physical senses too imprecise to register variations which, although seemingly minor, may have significant consequences. Long-term cycles of sunspot activity, increases in volcanic eruptions, atmospheric changes due to industrial or commercial activity—these can alter the climate with consequences that few appreciate. A one- or two-degree-Celsius increase or decrease in the earth's average temperature, a distinct possibility under a variety of circumstances, would dramatically alter the surface of the earth and human activity upon it.

Scientists occasionally call attention to climatic changes, and populations struggle and suffer individual and institutional stress because of those changes, but the attention the schools pay to the impacts of climatic change are hardly proportional to the importance of the matter. Middle-class American premises about time, nature, ownership, and the good life combine to make it very difficult to arouse interest in or concern about the significance of an expansion of the earth's deserts by a few hundred yards or similar, climate-related, long-term trends.

Tools

The relationship of technology to the human situation is one of the least-neglected areas of study of sociocultural systems. General histories usually include descriptions of at least a few technological innovations and their major social, political, or economic consequences, and occasionally entire college courses are devoted to the subject. Most students already know something of the effect on human society of the compass, cotton gin, computer, and other major inventions. In fact, technology as a factor in social change may receive so much attention that other causes of change my be eclipsed.

But widespread awareness of the role of technology in triggering change does not mean that the dynamic of the process is understood, or that its subtleties and ramifications are appreciated. What a good model offers beyond the usual discussion is a comprehensive means of tracing the *range* of effects of an innovation and the often-complex, many-stage causal sequence it triggers.

W. F. Cottrell's summary of the effects of the transition from steam to diesel locomotives during World War II illustrates the vast and varied consequences which can result from a single innovation. He describes how, in order to move the millions of tons of war materials needed overseas during the war, the United States found it necessary to build large numbers of ocean-going freighters. Many of these ships were designed for diesel engines, with the result that facilities for the production of diesels had to be rapidly and extensively expanded.

At the same time, the movement of goods and military personnel by rail within the United States was placing heavy demands on the available steam locomotives. Partly because large diesel engines were becoming available, and partly because diesels were cheaper to operate, steam locomotives began to be replaced by diesel units.

The social effects of this change were far-reaching. The pre–World War II locomotive demanded extensive routine maintenance. For some maintenance procedures, the locomotive had to be disconnected from the train, an operation that required men and equipment. Since the train had to stop anyway, cars were inspected and shunted into a shop for repair. These operations required additional men, heavy equipment, and facilities. Around these railroad service points towns grew, towns in which the largest payroll and the largest property taxes were paid by the railroad. With the railroad shops providing a seemingly secure economic base, political institutions were created, stores, banks, and other businesses were established, and populations expanded. Towns stabilized around the economy of the railroad.

But diesel locomotives changed everything. Needing far fewer stops for fuel and service, they passed through dozens of railroad towns without pausing. Railroad shops shut down, payrolls ended abruptly, and people moved away. Banks and other businesses closed their doors. Schools and churches were boarded up. Civic clubs disbanded, and lawyers, physicians, and other professionals established practices elsewhere. Many of the towns deserted by the railroads have never recovered.

The changes which accompanied the transition from steam to diesel locomotives were startlingly swift, but they were not unique. Indeed, it is difficult to think of a technological innovation that has not altered human society. In the analysis of the impacts of such changes, a comprehensive model helps pull thinking on from a preoccupation with the innovation itself to the kinds of consequences Cottrell describes. It can provide a framework that allows the student to do with any technological change what Cottrell has done. It can make far more apparent how change structures and restructures daily routine, creates individual and societal problems, renders skills and abilities obsolete, turns assets into liabilities, drives economic and psychological wedges between individuals and between groups, undermines institutional effectiveness, and generates vast social and psychological stress.

Wealth

According to an old saying, money cannot buy happiness. Perhaps not. But money can and does buy differing experiences, and those differing experiences can have a great deal to do not only with happiness but with much else of consequence.

In *People of Plenty*, David Potter points out some of the infant and childhood experiences a middle-class American level of wealth will buy:

— Birth and early care in a technologically complex hospital

— The technology and equipment for bottle feeding

— A separate crib or bed

— Diapers and other devices permitting permissive toilet training

— Warmth through space heating rather than by freedom-constricting swaddling

— A room of one's own

— Parents who have chosen when and how many children to have

— Separate housing, and therefore separation from grandparents and other members of the extended family

— Insulation from survival concerns (food, clothing, and shelter seem to appear "from nowhere")

— Exclusive ownership of toys and other objects

— Travel

— The services of doctors, dentists, music teachers, etc.

·It does not take too much perception to see relationships between these kinds of socialization experiences and some of the important values and ideas held by adult Americans. Deep-seated attitudes about individualism, freedom, equality, competitiveness, mobility, and democracy are consistent with, and no doubt have roots in, childhood experiences related to material abundance. In more subtle but equally powerful ways, differing levels of wealth within and between human societies help create differing conceptions of the self, of significant others, of time, space, causation, the good life, and of nearly every other cognitive system component. They also contribute to the formation of distinctive patterns of action, such as those for organizing families, associating, expressing creativity, controlling deviance, and making decisions.

What might be called "system wealth"—fluid assets which can flow rather freely between individuals and groups—is usually related to resources but is not the same thing. The fertile soil of North America was a resource to the colonists but of less value to the Indians. The colonists did little but grind grain with the water power that made the early industrialists wealthy, and the early industrialists had little use for the coal and oil upon which the economy was later dependent. As the Japanese have demonstrated, it is possible to generate enormous quantities of system wealth without much of a foundation of natural wealth.

The study of wealth—the total amount within a sociocultural system, its internal distribution, and its impact on personality, action patterns, and cultural premises—belongs in the curriculum.

Alien Organisms and Substances

Some scholar has maintained that, in ancient Rome, the poor used inexpensive pots and other utensils made of unglazed clay, while the wealthy ate and drank from glazed earthenware. It is theorized that the decline of Rome was in part attributable to the loss of its leadership as the affluent suffered the effects of poisoning from the lead used in the glazing process.

In 1349, the English issued an ordinance requiring that everyone work for the same pay as had been received in 1347. The ordinance established penalties for refusal to work, penalties for leaving a job to take another for higher pay, and penalties for employers who offered pay increases to employees. Parliament was attempting, unsuccessfully, to combat one of the effects of the Black Plague. So many workers had died that those who were left found themselves in an advantageous bargaining position. Some historians believe that the Plague was the major contributing factor in the elimination of feudalism.

When average scores on the Scholastic Aptitude Test began to decline in the 1960s, some researchers maintained that the principal factor in the decline was Iodine-131. The test takers, they said, had been born during the era of atmospheric testing of nuclear devices, and enough of the element had been absorbed to affect the thyroid gland's production of hormones controlling brain development.

Obviously, societies can be much altered by organisms and substances which change system components, thereby altering system balances. Sometimes the effects are immediate and obvious, as was the case when Ireland was struck by the potato blight. More often changes occur so gradually that they are not even noticed or become apparent so late that effective reaction is impossible. Asbestos fibers in the air, mercury in fish, lead in automobile exhaust gases, acid in rain, water hyacinth in lakes and rivers, food additives in the digestive system—we know about and watch at least some elements which can alter the ways systems function. We need a curriculum that makes formal provision for the monitoring of this sort of data and which broadens concern beyond the present preoccupation with impacts on health.

Information about the physical dimension occupied by a particular sociocultural system makes up the fourth part of our model. I will call this component "environment." The following categories encompass the major physical characteristics of sociocultural systems:

- Size
- Resources
- Constructions
- Wealth
- Tools
- Climate
- Topography
- Clothing
- Other systems
- Aesthetic creations
- Symbols
- Alien organisms and substances
- Language

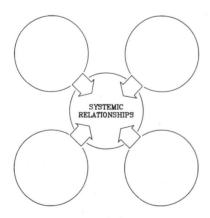

Systemic Relationships

There is an old Chinese riddle: If you have a horse and cart, how many things do you have? The answer? Three. A horse, a cart and a horse and a cart. I have discussed four aspects of sociocultural systems—demographics, environment, patterns of action, and cultural premises—but the four are five. The fifth component of study is the relationships between the four.

Relationships

To apply the first four components of the model to a sociocultural system, the system must be made to "stand still," must be frozen at some moment in time while the demographics are summarized, the environment inventoried, the patterns of action and states of mind described. But sociocultural systems do not stand still. They are constantly evolving and changing, sometimes rapidly and sometimes almost imperceptibly, but changing nonetheless. A key to understanding the nature and dynamics of this process of change is the identification and analysis of relationships between the four major components of sociocultural systems—relationships among actors, set, plot, and action. In the distinctive drama that unfolds within every society, each component has a reality of its own, but the play depends upon their interaction.

Before discussing the use of the model in the study of relationships, it is helpful to remember that the discovery of relationships is the second general step of a basic process by means of which human knowledge is expanded. The first step is the discernment of patterns—reaction patterns, growth patterns, behavior patterns, patterns on the oscilloscope, patterns of symptoms, patterns of response—any and all patterns. The second step is the determination of that to which the pattern relates. Temperature? Anxiety? Diet? Political persuasion? Impurities in the mix? Childhood trauma? Altitude? Planetary motion? Trust? Corrosion?

The infant discovers that crying brings attention. A relationship has been discovered and knowledge is expanded. The medical researcher finds that disease rates are significantly lower among those who take frequent, hot baths. A relationship has been discovered, and knowledge is expanded. During an extended period in Western history, several small segments of the population seemed to enjoy greater-than-average economic success. These same groups adhered to certain Protestant beliefs about the means to and evidence of eternal salvation. Max Weber argued that a relationship existed between the economic performance and the religious belief. Knowledge expanded. In the 1950s, Jane Jacobs began to point out that it was not always possible to identify a slum by appearance, that some very seedy-looking parts of some cities were in fact pleasant and safe places to live, and many brand new and visually attractive areas were unfulfilling, frustrating, even dangerous places in which to reside. The environment and the quality of life are related, she said, but not always in ways generally supposed. Knowledge was extended.

Check the lists of books considered to have been powerfully influential, books such as Tocqueville's *Democracy in America*, Rachel Carson's *Silent Spring*, Oliver Wendell Holmes's *The Contageousness of Puerpural Fever*, and

Mahan's *The Influence of Sea Power Upon History, 1660–1783*. More often than not, the books considered most significant will be those which point to the existence of a relationship not previously known, understood, or appreciated. From the work of the earliest systematic thinkers to the latest reports of research foundation, knowledge has advanced as relationships have been discovered.

Relationships are the product of a search for understanding; the source of answers to one of the most human of all questions: what is going on here? There are endless variations, but the basic question is the same: *what is going on here?* Why did the fire go out? Why does it thunder? Why did a candidate with his views not get elected? Why are these photographs grainier than usual? Why are the Dow-Jones averages declining? Why is this valve so sensitive to temperature variations? Why does the infection persist? Why are these students so highly motivated? These are the kinds of questions which stretch the mind and expand the frontiers of knowledge. And answering them requires the discovery of relationships.

Incidentally, why helping students learn to recognize, analyze, describe, and evaluate relationships is not ordinarily among the primary, formally stated objectives of education is a mystery. That it is generally not even mentioned as an objective is appalling. In many, perhaps most classes, the basic process by means of which knowledge is extended and understanding grows is largely ignored.

If knowledge of relationships is indeed central to understanding, it follows that (1) a knowledge of relationships having to do with sociocultural systems is central to an understanding of human experience, and (2) the expansion of knowledge about sociocultural systems requires the identification and exploration of relationships. What then becomes necessary is some means of identifying what it is about and within sociocultural systems that can be significantly related. The model serves that purpose. By identifying the major components of sociocultural systems, it provides the raw materials of relationships—elements which can be combined in myriad ways to suggest potentially useful explanations and insights. For example:

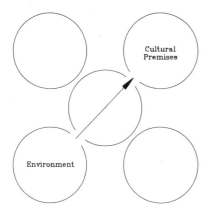

Assignment: Explore possible relationships between the nature of a human system's weapons and shared conceptions of the self within that system.

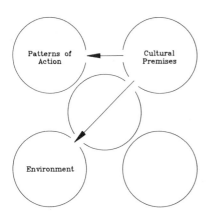

Assignment: Identify and discuss possible relationships between shared assumptions about the nature of the future and the rate and direction of currency flow in unregulated economies.

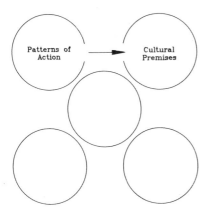

Assignment: What sort of relationship, if any, does there seem to be between the difficulty of getting into an organization and dedication to that organization once one has become a member?

As the model demonstrates, every level of generality of relationship can be explored. Here is an example of a relationship expressed at three different levels of generality:

ENVIRONMENT	RELATES TO	PATTERNS OF ACTION
ENVIRONMENT (RESOURCES)	RELATES TO	PATTERNS (FOR DISTRIBUTING WEALTH)
ENVIRONMENT (RESOURCES) (Wood, major energy source in ancient Rome, increasingly distant and costly)	RELATES TO	PATTERNS (FOR DISTRIBUTING WEALTH: widening gap between rich and poor)

This same example also illustrates the model's range and flexibility. If, for example, it is known that wood was indeed a major energy source for ancient Rome, and that over the centuries it became increasingly difficult and costly to obtain, that fact can be treated as a given and every other component of the model "checked out" to identify significant relationships. The entry in the right-hand column is simply removed and replaced with another drawn from the model. Did the energy situation affect demographics—the distribution and density of members, for example? Did it alter the environment—its size through territorial acquisition? Its use? Other resources? The design of structures? Technology? What about action patterns other than those for the distribution of wealth? Did the energy situation affect patterns for work? For status? Family organization? Making decisions? Did changes in the availability of energy alter in any way Roman cultural premises? Conceptions of the good life? Ideas about significant others? Self? Time orientation?

The same procedure can be followed with the other component of the original relationship statement. If one knows that in ancient Rome's later years the income gap between rich and poor tended to widen, every other component of the model is available as a source of possible explanatory hypotheses.

It really makes little difference now how wide the range of incomes of Rome's citizens or what their energy problems may have been. But at a higher level of generality those same propositions may be important and useful. Once it has been demonstrated that the demographics, environment, patterns of action, and cultural premises of a sociocultural system are related, and that the sources, characteristics, and availability of energy do indeed affect human societies in any number of significant ways, the resultant complex of model-generated concepts can be applied to sociocultural systems which *are* important—one's own and those with which one must coexist.

Incidentally, it should not take more than a few minutes of this kind of play with the model to see just how arbitrary and limiting the traditional disciplines can be. The search for useful relationships may lead anywhere. To channel students into courses and programs which erect artificial boundaries between closely related parts of reality does them a real and permanent disservice.

Change

It is the easiest of steps from a study of relationships within sociocultural systems to a study of the dynamics of change within those systems. A relationship statement reads "A is related to B." To begin an exploration of social change, the statement is simply extended to "A change in one will probably affect the other." If one's model for study identifies the major elements of sociocultural systems, then a consideration of changes in relationships within and between those elements will provide a comprehensive tool for the study of change.

We need such a tool, and it should begin to be built in the earliest years of education. That social change, a movement so related to everyday life, so omnipresent, so powerful, so much a factor in the effort to achieve individual and collective stability and happiness, is paid so little attention in the classroom is incredible. In the study of sociocultural systems, indeed in all study, it is difficult to imagine anything of greater importance than an understanding of the forces which shape our daily experience and our destinies.

SOCIAL CHANGE: PATTERNS OF ACTION AND CULTURAL PREMISES. Dirty looks, burning books, ridicule, prison, banishment, head shaving, asylums, ostracism, hanging, the threat of Hell—in all societies the weapons devised for use against those who appear to threaten the status quo are numerous, varied, and often ingenious. In Roman-occupied territory, those who questioned the established order were sometimes crucified. Among the Amish, an individual who fails to conform to accepted practices may be shunned, may go for months or years without being spoken to by family or friends. In parts of southern India, a man who "looks at young and beautiful girls and describes their dresses and shapes" can expect in the afterlife to be "nailed to the wall with sharp nails and then thrown into melting limestone and have limewater thrown into his eyes." Even small children are often cruel to those whose actions or ideas are perceived as different. History books contain any number of accounts of individuals who met untimely ends because they appeared to threaten established patterns of action or premises. Many school boards across the United

States once spent much time trying to decide what to do about male students who came to school without belts in their trousers.

All societies have two treasures, threats to which are almost certain to bring defensive measures swinging into action. One of these treasures is its patterns of action—the accepted way of organizing families, distributing wealth, associating, and other patterns we have identified. The other treasure is the cluster of assumptions identified in the model as "cultural premises."

The treasures have guardians: the Elders, the Klan, the Village Council, the Censor, the Citizens for a Safer Athens, the Un-American Activities Committee. In every sociocultural system, in every era, the ultimate threat is "the threat to our way of life." "Our way of life" means "our patterns of action and our cultural premises."

Despite efforts to keep them unchanged, a system's patterns of action and its shared premises are not static. They evolve, and they are sometimes deliberately changed to make them more consistent with each other (as when racial patterns in America's schools were changed in the 1950s to more closely align them with an American premise about human equality). But the evolution is usually slow, the change reluctant. Very little change occurs within sociocultural systems because members desire it. What may at first appear to be a deliberate move in a new direction is more likely, when studied closely, to be a mere course correction designed to restore, insulate, or maintain prevailing action patterns and premises. Both tend to be static.

SYSTEM CHANGE: DEMOGRAPHICS AND THE ENVIRONMENT. Sociocultural systems do not ordinarily change because those within them are unhappy with their own ideas and ways of acting and deliberately set out to alter them. Nevertheless, ideas and ways of acting do change, often very rapidly, and in directions which are often not to the liking of those within the system.

One might assume that changes which come about despite their general unpopularity must surely be imposed, that a powerful elite or a militarily superior neighbor is responsible. That is not generally the case. In fact, direct threats often result not in change but in an increased attachment to traditional patterns and premises. As many conquerors have discovered, physical force is a very poor tool for bringing about desired social change. Shielded by doors or codes, traditional ways may defy forceful change for decades or centuries.

Then what are the sources of change? Why is it that, despite deliberate resistance, patterns of action and cultural premises change nevertheless? The answer lies primarily in characteristics inherent in the demographics and environment components of the model. The natural tendency of patterns of action and cultural premises is to be static. Demographics and the environment, on the other hand, tend to be dynamic, unstable, even uncontrollable.

And since sociocultural systems are true systems, the inevitable and uncontrollable changes within components of demographics and environment alter patterns of action and cultural premises despite concerted and often organized efforts to resist.

The instability of most components of demographics and environment is inherent. There is, for example, no practical way acceptable to the members of most societies to achieve and maintain absolutely zero population growth. Population is therefore always increasing or decreasing, and either trend triggers other changes throughout the system. (Some societies have so geared their institutions to population growth that zero population growth itself creates change.)

The number of members of a system cannot be rigidly controlled; neither can there be effective control over the relative size of various age groupings, the balance of males to females, the climate, the available resources, the reshaping of the earth by nature, or any other category within demographics and environment. Even within highly totalitarian societies controlled by leaders who appreciate the destabilizing effects of change and attempt to "freeze" various change factors, major change is inevitable. Rigid enforcement of a pass system to control citizen movement may briefly maintain existing population patterns, or a particular technological innovation may be destroyed or outlawed, but no strategy works for long.

And even if some way could be devised to arrest one or two change factors, some are simply beyond human regulation. When a long-term weather cycle that has brought adequate rain to an area for many years comes to an end, there is going to be social change. Nothing can be done to stop it. Alternative sources of water may be found, but the very process of switching to those alternatives will create change. The use of irreplaceable resources has the same effect. When an oil field has been pumped dry it is dry. The earth has one less oil field forever. The change is irreversible. Soon or late, the consequences are going to ripple through those human systems which have anything either directly or indirectly to do with oil.

Changes in the demographic characteristics and in the environment of sociocultural systems are inevitable. And, because patterns of action and cultural premises have usually grown out of, and are therefore related to, those characteristics, they cannot remain unaffected. If patterns for work are based upon the supply of fish in the river and the fish disappear, the old pattern must either be abandoned or become ritual. Either way, the pattern for work has changed. If premises about the good life are based on an economy of abundance and the depletion of resources dictates an economy of scarcity, the old premises about what constitutes the good life will either change or those who hold them will be miserable or considered mentally ill.

The second reason why changes within the components of demographics and environment have such tremendous power to trigger other changes is that they generally occur below the threshhold of awareness of most members of the sociocultural systems affected. Few societies have either the means to measure or an interest in keeping precise data on what is happening within each of the components. Americans, for example, pay a great deal of attention to events which unfold more or less instantaneously—the hijacking, the court decision, the exposure of an instance of corruption, the eruption of a volcano. But cumulative events, those made up of myraid actions or instances stretching over intervals of time, generally receive little or no attention. An oil spill with a temporarily adverse effect on a body of water will almost always draw the helicopters of the news services. But when individual drops of oil from automobile engine crankcases and transmissions collect on the surface of parking lots, then wash into storm sewers and do equal damage to the same body of water, there may be no interest or reaction at all.

Changes in demographics and environment tend to be all but invisible. The medical researcher whose work will lengthen life expectancy by several weeks is not trying to subvert the social security system, create another Sun City in Florida, or increase the political power of senior citizens. Alone in the laboratory, the researcher is simply trying to solve a problem, meet a challenge, and earn a salary and perhaps a laudatory article in a medical journal. The cascading consequences of the work being done—the changes in neighborhoods, in taxes, in medical costs, and in much else—will be below most citizens' level of awareness.

Individual decisions to have a child, to move to another place, to drill a water well, to buy a wood-burning space heater, or to travel abroad make no headlines and attract no particular notice, but when these actions are replicated thousands or millions of times, the cumulative effect is almost always far more significant than are most of the events which do make the headlines. We often pay no attention at all to cumulative events, not until the river is completely dead, the economy is foundering, the faucets run dry, or the desert reaches our doors. When the situation is finally noted, social changes to adequately cope with the problems create stresses which wrench and twist the society, or else the necessary changes are of such a magnitude that there is an unwillingness even to attempt them.

There is nothing particularly complex or mysterious about the basic processes of social change. Most upper-elementary-aged children can take each of the components of demographics and environment and point out at least some of the pressures which changes in them exert on other aspects of the whole. Unfortunately, American society (perhaps because the schools have little or nothing to say on the subject and thereby imply that it is not important) functions on the basis of considerably simpler conceptions of the dynamics of change. There is some appreciation of the power of technological innovation (Congress, for example, has an Office of Technological Assessment), but the operant view is that human intent is the major cause of change. Presidents, kings, Congress, or Communists are considered responsible for what happens. This assumption, largely a legacy of an earlier time when those in power commissioned the only written record of events, is reinforced by most American history textbooks, and by the mass media. Things happen, according to this view, because people make them happen.

There is another, less tangible assumption about social change that can be found in some segments of American society—a generalized feeling that what happens is not the result of complex (but understandable) factors but is instead a product of forces or plans which are of other than earthly origin. There is, of course, no way to know whether or not this belief is valid, but to the extent that it pervades the thinking of Americans, to that extent other possible explanations of social change are irrelevant and an understanding of them is unnecessary. Those who subscribe to this view perceive social change primarily in moral terms. Society, they often feel, used to be more virtuous, possessed of greater moral fiber. Institutions such as the family used to be stronger and more stable, held together by the sheer goodness of the members. Wherever Rome went, they believe, modern society is also going. Our collective success or failure, growth or decline, survival or extinction is thought to hinge primarily upon our response to moral questions. "Good" societies flourish; "bad" ones die.

If this is not the whole story, and earthly factors play an important role in social change, then each of the components of demographics and environment needs to be understood and monitored. This is true, of course, because sociocultural systems are very much true systems. Changes within them are systemic rather than linear. Once the change process is in motion (as it always has been), everything interacts with everything else. Each component is both cause and effect, end and beginning, acting and acted upon, and every facet of life is woven into the process and is altered by that fact.

INTEGRATION. Sociocultural systems are true systems. The various components and characteristics tend to fit together. Action patterns, cultural premises, demographics, and environment exhibit a degree of consistency and are to a considerable extent mutually supportive. In the United States, for example, conceptions of the self as a separate, independent entity without organic ties to an extended family or clan mesh with the patterns for work and the distribution of wealth. Since free enterprise requires a very mobile labor supply—individuals willing and able to move quickly and easily from one area to another—it can be seen that middle-class American conceptions of the self mesh with the demands of the work pattern.

However, primarily because of factors related to social change, various aspects of sociocultural systems often do not integrate smoothly. Stress of one kind or another then results. For example, middle-class Americans place a high value on autonomy, on a state loosely called "freedom," on being one's "own boss." Meshing with this assumption of what is best and proper are several patterns, including those for making decisions. In the political realm, there is democracy and the vote. In religion, there are many denominations, widespread use of congregational forms of governance, and the option not to participate at all. In many families, there is discussion and shared decision making. These patterns are consistent with cultural premises.

But in other areas of American life the patterns are not consistent with cultural premises. Premises about the self do not integrate with patterns for decision making generally used in American industry, education, and other institutions. Workplace organization traditionally derives from military models and tends to be authoritarian and hierarchical, with little provision for shared decision making. The result is that, for many Americans, work is indeed work. Deepseated negative feelings about it are verified by studies which indicate elevated levels of stress with consequent physical and psychological costs. On the other hand, organizations and industries which do attempt to achieve a greater consistency between prevailing premises and decision making, those which adopt Theory Y or Z management philosophies, flatten organizational hierarchy, minimize status differences in facilities, and establish procedures for open communication, are generally happier, more productive, and profitable.

The degree of integration of the various components of sociocultural systems is constantly changing. Very generally speaking, demographic and environmental pressures tend to push system components apart, while effort stemming from cultural premises is directed toward greater integration. The picture is complex, but the model helps organize the study of internal consistencies and inconsistencies by identifying appropriate "pieces" of the systems and allowing them to be easily juxtaposed so that students can identify problems and sources of stress not yet part of general public consciousness.

This discussion of relationships and change adds a fifth major component to the model. I will call this component "systemic relationships and change." I have also added the phrase *dynamic tendency* within the demographic and environment components of the model, and *static tendency* within patterns of action and cultural premises.

A graphic representation of the completed model is below. Although it lacks graphic devices indicating the nearly-infinite possibilities for juxtaposing concepts and exploring their relationships, the following figure is nevertheless probably the most important illustration in the book. It presents the same conceptual model previously represented by five circles, but in a form illustrating that it is indeed possible for a single conceptual structure to encompass all the traditional academic disciplines and logically relate all the content of general education. In this version, the concept of sociocultural system occupies the first column on the left. To its right are the four sub-concepts essential to its understanding. Each column elaborates, in turn, the column to its left. (Beyond the third column, space limitations make it possible to show only a few examples of appropriate curriculum content.) Conceptual structuring appropriate for instruction comes not, of course, from an ability to fill in the thousands of indicated conceptual components, but in the discernment of major conceptual categories and category relationships.

It may seem that I have arrived at this model in arbitrary or idiosyncratic fashion. This is not the case. Several different approaches to the task of building a model for the study of societies lead to this particular construct. Perhaps the most direct begins with a definition of the concept of a sociocultural system. When one looks at obviously coherent systems and asks what it is that delineates them and ensures that one is observing a unified whole, a simple statement emerges: *A sociocultural system is a collection of people who occupy the same general area, act in similar ways, and share important states of mind.* From this definition, one can construct the five-element model.

— Demographics (a collection of people)

— Environment (occupy the same general area)

— Patterns of action (act in similar ways)

— Cultural premises (share important states of mind)

— Systemic relationships and change (relationships between the above four)

Alternatively, one can look at work within cultural anthropology, archeology, macrosociology, history, and human geography—the disciplines traditionally most concerned with the holistic study of human societies—and find in one school of thought or another a major interest in the kind of information encompassed by each of the components of the model.

For those who have little interest in or inclination toward systematic studies, or who react negatively to the social sciences, it may be helpful to point out that, within the humanities, two major forms regularly model human

SOCIOCULTURAL SYSTEM

DEMOGRAPHICS

- Number
- Age
- Sex
- Density
- Distribution
- Capacities, capabilities

dynamic tendency

ENVIRONMENT

- Location
- Size, shape
- Topography
- Climate
- Tools
- Constructions
- Resources
- Wealth
- Language
- Clothing
- Art
- Symbols
- Alien organisms, substances
- Other systems

PATTERNS OF ACTION

- Worship
- Work
- Making decisions
- Controlling behavior
- Educating
- Distr., exchanging wealth
- Maintaining membership
- Owning
- Status
- Controlling boundaries
- Communicating
- Esthetic expression
- Social service
- Play
- Special days

static tendency

CULTURAL PREMISES

- Causation
- Nature
- Time
- Space
- Self
- Supernatural
- Acceptable, unaccept. action
- Meaning of existence
- Significant others
- The good life
- Trends

Producing
Distributing
Fighting
Monitoring
Health maintaining
Transporting
Communicating
Entertaining

Capture
Kill
Incapacitate
Cut support
Terrorize

Adoption of aliens
Sexual union
Immigration
Conquest

Child bearing
Marriage
Courtship
Pairing

Value
Structure
Stages
Rhythms
Boundaries

Integrated
Multi-faceted
Fragmented

experience using the same five components of this model. As I pointed out in an early chapter note, both drama and the novel use actors or characters (demographics), a stage or setting (environment), a plot (cultural premises), and action (patterns of action). The finished drama or story traces the interaction of these elements (systemic relationships and change).

Let me repeat, for emphasis, the arguments earlier presented in support of the concept of sociocultural system as the core of the general education curriculum:

1. They are the most comprehensive systems we know, and are therefore capable of organizing and logically relating enormous quantities of seemingly disparate information.

2. Each of us is a child of one of them, and we cannot really know ourselves unless we know our origins.

3. In our attempt to understand reality, they structure all our perceptions.

4. They are the basic units of human organization.

5. They order our every meaningful action and thought, and only if we are consciously aware of that ordering are we able, if we choose, to be free of it.

6. The academic disciplines, even mathematics and science, are bounded and biased by them.

7. Survival requires awareness of options for organizing life, and other systems are the richest source of such options.

8. They are everywhere, some of them are very powerful, and ignorance of their structure and functioning can be costly and dangerous.

The model for the study of sociocultural systems I am suggesting is, of course, only one of many which could be used to integrate and elaborate the general education curriculum. If it is considered inadequate, then another could be devised. An earlier comment bears repeating: knowledge is neither more nor less than the power to manipulate the world according to the principles inherent in the particular model used to represent it.

It is sociocultural systems we must come to understand. In that effort, it is not a question of choosing or not choosing to use models. There is no alternative to their use. The only choice is between models of various quality, between models unexamined and unevaluated and those which are the product of deliberate, careful thought.

Chapter 3

Integrating Knowledge

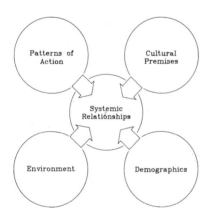

Procedural Problems

The study of humanness is central to humanness, and sociocultural systems, for the reasons I have noted, are the logical focus of such study. A formal, systematic study of these systems can integrate knowledge and the general education curriculum, strengthen the traditional academic disciplines, and identify presently neglected areas of knowledge.

Our concern is to lay out a conceptual foundation for the general education curriculum based on a model for the concept of culture, to demonstrate its comprehensiveness and practicality, and to show its potential for the improvement of instruction. I do not believe that there is any likelihood of significant change in the general education curriculum, but a few observations in passing about such change may be appropriate.

Reform should begin with the tentative adoption of a model of sociocultural systems, including all concepts, subconcepts, and conceptual relationships which collectively provide a framework for the description and analysis of socio-cultural systems. Levels of generality and abstractness should be established, and optimum sequences and rates of instruction determined. Relevant traditional content should then be integrated, new content developed for important but presently neglected areas of study, and instructional materials created and tied to levels of learner ability and maturity. The end result should be a sequential, increasingly complex study of at least ten or twelve years' duration extending from elementary school through prespecialization work at the university level.

It would take several years to build such a program. During this period social studies at the elementary and secondary levels and perhaps cultural anthropology courses at the college level would be adequate vehicles for experimentation and testing. Social studies is in dire need of reorganization anyway, for its preoccupation with particularistic information rather than con-ceptually focused instruction has brought it to a chaotic state. Indeed, in its present form social studies is not an academic discipline at all. It is an incredible heap of miscellany—some odd pieces of the past held together by habit, a few bits of several social sciences (themselves in need of major rethinking), the remnants of a dozen ill-digested fads, an assortment of responses to demands of state legislators and special interest groups, and other odds and ends assigned to social studies because they have not seemed to fit anywhere else. The adoption of a conceptual approach focusing on sociocultural systems would alter some social studies course content and put a different emphasis on other content, but no administrative changes would be required. Course schedules and titles could remain as they are, thereby enormously simplifying the change process.

Although a total restructuring of the general education curriculum would be a major undertaking, the first step toward such a curriculum—refining a theoretical framework similar to the model I have proposed—should not be difficult. Establishing an instructional sequence and preparing teaching materials based on the framework would take time and money, but by federal or even state standards this aspect of the project would certainly be manageable.

The really difficult task would be that of reaching individual teachers. Most have grown up "thinking small," concerned primarily with a fragment of the whole of knowledge and unaccustomed to relating that fragment to much else. A great many teachers have both a rationale for and a vested interest in things as they presently are, and would feel threatened by change, particularly by change they sincerely believed was unnecessary.

School administrators could be keys to the eventual development of a more defensible curriculum, but reaching them might be even more difficult than reaching classroom teachers. In American schools, many of those in administrative positions have come to those positions by way of athletics or other marginally academic paths. They often have neither background nor interest in curriculum theory and design. In fact, if what publishers say about most school administrators' reading habits is true, it may be that a majority do not have a general interest in education. Perhaps understandably, their primary interest is in the smooth functioning of the institutions for which they are responsible, and changes are often resisted unless they are seen as necessary to avoid adverse public reaction. Like many classroom teachers, then, but for different reasons, many administrators are likely to be threatened by change.

It is possible that with enough time and money strategies could be devised which would overcome at least some teacher and administrator resistance. However, the difficulties should not be underestimated. It should also be borne in mind that school boards, testing agencies, legislatures, and many other powerful groups feel most comfortable with things as they are. Even when there is a willingness to change, the goal is clear, and all participants are enthusiastic, the near paralysis of educational bureaucracies makes the task exceedingly difficult.

Somewhat more likely than a major federal or state effort to rethink general education would be an effort within a small system or single institution to achieve at least some of the benefits of a coherent, integrated curriculum. Small pilot programs would be entirely feasible. It would be difficult for a small-scale effort to produce a sophisticated, vertically articulated program spanning several years, but at the secondary and college level a cluster of integrated courses could certainly be assembled.

The essentials for success are relatively few. Since the task would be primarily intellectual in nature, a large budget should not be necessary. Far more important would be a supportive administration and a design team of able teachers secure enough in their roles to probe the infrequently examined premises which underlie their fields. Simply holding up those premises to the scrutiny of team members from other disciplines would be a healthy beginning. An important second task would be writing content-specific instructional objectives not tied to individual disciplines, objectives equally appropriate for each of the represented disciplines.

Team members could begin the actual curriculum-building process by agreeing on a conceptual framework that would guide the study of sociocultural systems and then designing an introductory instructional course based on the framework. The potential benefits of this activity are so great that the task should probably be undertaken even if there is no intent to schedule a separate introductory course. The establishment of shared objectives, vocabulary, and meanings, the clarification and refinement of concepts and concept relationships, an awareness of the whole so that each discipline's role is kept in perspective—these needs can be met only if there is extensive dialogue. When instruction begins, teachers can return to their individual rooms, but the shared experience of designing a comprehensive knowledge structure would make possible team teaching at its best.

Exploring new conceptual territory and reworking the curriculum to encompass that territory could be an exceedingly rich experience. And, because some of the territory would be genuinely new, many of the usual problems which accompany attempts to integrate content (problems stemming from the tendency to use one's own discipline as the point of orientation) should be less likely to appear. The professional growth that can result from cooperative, creative activity is often startling, and the benefits to school and students are almost always immediately apparent.

A few dozen systemwide projects around the country would certainly enjoy the kind of success that attracts attention and imitation. For many of the reasons already noted, however, change at this level is difficult also. And, until there is general appreciation of the fundamental inadequacy of present approaches to the selection and organization of knowledge, such local projects are unlikely to be undertaken.

At the present time, then, changes in what is taught in the schools are most likely to come from individual teachers. There are, of course, difficulties at this level also. Anyone who has worked with a number of teachers is familiar with the now-traditional "What you're talking about is a good idea, but . . . ," "It doesn't apply to my field," "It isn't appropriate at the level I teach," "I'm already doing it," "It won't work with *my* students," "The administration wouldn't allow it," "Adequate instructional materials aren't available," or "I owe it to my students to prepare them for the standard exams."

Resistance also comes from the assumption that present subjects and disciplines are based on polished, tightly reasoned, comprehensive conceptual structures carefully designed and handed down by some ancient supermind. Memories of classroom activity from earlier years, the impressive slickness of textbooks, the near standardization of tables of content, and the tendency to see great value in what is known and little value in what is not all combine to make teacher questioning of the structure of the traditional academic disciplines seem presumptuous. Most resist the idea that the disciplines they know so well, the disciplines through which they have come to organize reality, are, more often than not, jerry-built, haphazardly organized, conceptually disjointed, and narrow.

But of course not everyone resists change. And, although teachers no longer have a great deal of latitude for independent action, and what little we do have is being steadily eroded, ingenious teachers can find ways to meet the traditional expectations (and often meet them better) while simultaneously pursuing more sophisticated and worthwhile educational goals.

There are, of course, major limitations on what individual teachers can do. We cannot, in very brief periods of time, help students acquire the depth of understanding of conceptual structures and relationships with other disciplines which is possible when ideas have been years in the forming. We cannot move with the students through the rest of their daily schedules, exploring those relationships with other disciplines which explain, enlarge, and reinforce. Nor can we reorganize the school's curriculum to reflect more logical divisions in the structure of knowledge.

What concerned teachers *can* at least do is place their disciplines in perspective. We have noted that each field of study in the general education curriculum is most of all an attempt to answer the question, What's going on here? Teachers can build a solid base for the discipline being presented by helping students see that what is going on is in large measure an appearance reflecting their culture. We can also demonstrate that what may seem isolated and simple is in fact integrally linked to much else and therefore complex, and we can clarify the nature and implications of at least some of these links. No matter what approach to instruction is adopted, these are surely essential.

It may be helpful to briefly survey several traditional academic disciplines and point up some of the implications of deliberately approaching them as parts of a larger, integrated whole. We will be saying, in essence, "Here is a comprehensive map of the concept of culture. Locate yourself and your discipline on it, and the benefits to you, your students, and the larger society will eventually surpass all your expectations."

The Model and Traditional Academic Disciplines

History

Perhaps in part because historians have promised more from the study of history than the study usually delivers, the perceived importance of the discipline has declined over the last several decades. It is still, however, a mainstay of the curriculum. Students are exposed to it rather relentlessly, and great faith is placed in its ability to do something educationally meritorious. Advertising brochures for history textbooks say that the study of history will "provide a sense of the past," or that it will give insight into "the roots of the contemporary situation." "Making the past come alive" is also often cited as a desirable outcome of study.

That there is value in these kinds of objectives of historical study is indisputable. What is far from certain, however, is whether what actually happens in history classrooms does indeed make the past come alive, provide a sense of it, or give insight into the roots of the contemporary situation. There is considerable evidence, some of it the product of formal research, that in fact nothing much at all of lasting consequence results from most students' several years' exposure to historical information. It is often argued that the benefits of such study are too subtle to evaluate, but the argument is not a very strong one. If the supposed benefits come from a knowledge of past events, and few of those events can be recalled by the average individual once the threat of examination no longer looms, it is difficult to support the claim that the study of history is of lasting value.

Three textbook-style sentences may help clarify some of the characteristics of traditional approaches to history instruction:

> The Americans signed, in 1783, a treaty with England recognizing the independence of the United States. England agreed to the generous treaty because, being at war with three countries at that moment, it decided to end the American drain on its military strength.
>   A war cannot, by itself, solve all the issues that bring it on. Americans soon found

Look again at the first sentence. In it the author takes several facts and puts them together to tell about something that happened. "The Americans signed, in 1783, a treaty with England recognizing the independence of the United States." Such actions are called "events," and the description of them makes up most of the traditional study of history. The usual account of an event describes somebody (Americans) who sometime (1783), somewhere (in this case, not stated), did something (signed a treaty). More advanced textbooks differ chiefly in the amount of elaboration of this same basic information—the participants in the event are named, the exact date and place are given, and the terms of the treaty are spelled out. The second of the three sentences gives a reason for the human activity described in the first sentence, and the third sentence states a generalization related to the whole matter.

This approach to the past as a learning resource—selecting certain aspects of it and arranging them to create a story—is the basis for most classroom instruction. Unfortunately, the approach is rarely effective, for the characteristics of historical narrative which give it potential power and vitality happen to be the same characteristics which are generally unacceptable to those who choose textbooks. In telling a story well, style is almost everything. Textbooks, however, can have no apparent style. They must appear to have been written by a computer. All the characteristics which usually make a story appealing—the idiosyncracies of the teller, the subjectivity, the undisguised speculation, the overstatement, the emotional peaks, the humor—are edited out. They are "inappropriate" for textbooks. What is left, in the well-known words of the historian Beard, is a history that is mostly "one damned thing after another."

Historical narrative is at least twenty-five centuries old. It may have begun with Herodotus, but probably goes back even earlier. It deserves a place in the curriculum, but it should be freed from the superficial, inadequately-thought-out constraints which push subjectivity below the surface and rob the story of its vitality. A good tale, well told, is much like a musical composition. Its value lies beyond rational explanation. It is good because it is interesting or beautiful or inspirational, good not because of what it helps us know but in how it makes us feel. Writing that arouses emotions is certainly an acceptable part of instruction. We need to recognize this role of history and allow certain kinds of history textbooks to be *more* subjective, *more* dramatic, *more* powerful, *more* inspiring (and less weighed down by the threat of final examination questions about countless details which meet no conceivable educational purpose of consequence). Reading or listening to a good story is an esthetic experience. There is no more reason to encumber that experience with a requirement that the details be memorized than there is to require that those who listen to symphonies be able to hum them afterward before it will be granted that their listening experience has been successful.

The past is a very rich resource. To attempt to merely make it come alive, to acquire some sense of it, or to seek in it only the roots of the contemporary situation is to make minimal use of its potential. As filmmakers and a few teachers demonstrate, it can be a source of great stories. But to pursue only the narrow objectives which are possible when it is organized in story form is an enormous waste. The past can be a major source of understanding—can help us better know our individual selves, the societies of which we are a part, and those with whom we must deal. Knowledge of the past can expand our freedoms and stimulate our creativity, can, in fact, contribute in very specific and very powerful ways to the achievement of every major objective of general education. But it cannot do so if narrative is the only form in which it is presented to students.

For a simple illustration of other problems with the narrative form of historical study, look once again at the three textbook sentences quoted earlier:

> The Americans signed, in 1783, a treaty with England recognizing the independence of the United States. England agreed to the generous treaty because, being at war with three countries at that moment, it decided to end the American drain on its military strength.

> A war cannot, by itself, solve all the issues that bring it on.

I have pointed out that the first sentence describes an event, and that descriptions of events make up most traditional historical accounts. Our familiarity with this way of writing about the past encourages us to assume that what the author was describing was, from a scholarly point of view, about the only thing of consequence taking place at the time. It is very easy to overlook the fact that a nearly infinite number of events occurred in America in 1783. Why a particular one was chosen to be described is far more difficult to explain and justify than one might suppose. It is more difficult to explain and justify than many historians suppose. History is not *the* story of the past, then, but merely *a* story of the past.

The late historian Carroll Quigley of the Georgetown School of Foreign Service observed the following in the introduction to his book, *The Evolution of Civilizations:*

> If historians are not explicit, at least to themselves, about their principles of selection among the facts of the past and among the many possible arrangement of these facts, all histories will be simply accidental compilations that cannot be justified in any rational way. Historians will continue to write about some of the events of history while neglecting others equally significant or even more significant, and they will form patterns for these facts along lines determined by traditional (and basically accidental) lines or in reflection of old controversies about the patterns of these facts. This, indeed, is pretty much what we have today.

The account that makes it into the pages of the textbook may have an aura of objectivity about it, but it is there either because the author selected it using very subjective and probably ill-defined criteria, or because a similar story has usually been included in other history textbooks. Neither reason is sufficiently compelling to justify the emphasis often placed on students being able to remember and recite information about most past events.

The second sentence of our textbook quote also raises important questions about the legitimacy and usefulness of the usual narrative style of history. In it, the author "explains" an event: "England agreed to the generous treaty because, being at war with three countries at that moment, it decided to end the American drain on its military strength." History textbooks contain so many statements like this one, and we have become so accustomed to them, that we hardly notice their superficiality. In a casual reading the statement sounds plausible enough, but it really does not explain very much at all. Why, for example, did not England quit fighting the other two countries and save its strength for the struggle with America? Almost certainly the decision was based on many factors, and perhaps could be traced to misinformation, the influence of various individuals and groups, a general lack of public enthusiasm for the war, or any number of other reasons or combination of reasons. This sort of casual approach to "explaining" why particular historical events occurred recurs constantly in conventional history textbooks.

The third sentence—"A war cannot, by itself, solve all the issues that bring it on"—sounds very much like a flat statement of fact. The author does not say, "In my opinion, etc." Without saying so directly, he or she seems to be maintaining that "history" has proven the statement true. Now it cannot be known for certain that the author's claim is *not* true, but it does appear that the whole question is being treated rather carelessly. Such a sweeping generalization surely needs more support than a mere citing of experience following a single war. We often accept in history books propositions we would not think of accepting in our newspapers or even in our students' papers.

Regarding the lack of rigor on the part of writers of narrative history, the late David Potter, Coe Professor of American History at Yale, wrote in the introduction to *People of Plenty:*

> In its headlong, ad hoc assault upon the record of human experience, history has built its narrative upon an extraordinary melange of unstated premises, random assumptions, untested hypotheses, and miscellaneous notions about the nature of man, the workings of society, and the causation of historical change. The anomalous nature of this conceptual foundation has scarcely been recognized by historians, much less confronted by them.

It may appear that a contradiction is present in the last several pages. On the one hand, I am saying that there should be a place in the curriculum for opinionated, subjective, stylized historical writing. On the other hand, an excerpt from a textbook is criticized because of its subjectivity. But I am recommending two very different uses of the past, neither of which resembles textbook-style history. The first use I have already discussed—history as narrative, as an exciting story, excitingly told, as a moving story, movingly told. The other approach is hardly concerned with narrative at all. It makes use of the past not to create an esthetic experience but to meet the whole range of general education objectives, to enormously expand the scope of historical study, and to tie history to the other academic disciplines. For these purposes, narrative history is inadequate. It is too "thin"; it traces too narrow a path through the past, leaves far too much uninvestigated, leans too much on the interests and judgement of too few individuals, who, by the very act of writing about the past for some present end, assert an interest in interpreting it in particular ways.

The model opens the door to an array of alternative approaches to the study of the past. All are valid, and many are of far greater usefulness in the search for an understanding of self, of situation, and of the human condition than the approaches presently employed.

For the teacher who would explore some of these alternatives, however, there is an initial question that must be faced: What about the traditional course content? A schedule that calls for the teaching of five sections of American history punctuated at intervals by the usual battery of standardized tests seems to allow little room for deviation from present practice.

What is to be done? Given the present conviction (particularly strong in American history) that mere exposure to the traditional stories has some significant positive effect, there is no alternative to their presentation. Paul Revere must ride, the Monitor and Merrimac must duel to a draw, and Roosevelt must ride up San Juan Hill. Any value of the model notwithstanding, the teacher who wishes to continue teaching must either tell these traditional stories or assign the appropriate pages in the textbook. Defensible or not, the expectations of society and the users of standardized tests must be met.

Can the model and the familiar accounts be made to mesh, the model organizing the stories and the stories explicating the model? The two can be married, but it is not a simple union. The model asks for far more than the stories offer, and the randomness and emptiness of many of the stories make it pointless to systematize them using the model. The teacher who is familiar with both the model and traditional accounts will move back and forth between them easily and constantly and find such movement useful, but a course of study formalizing such a process would probably not be worth the trouble its creation would require. The traditional stories must be presented, the model opens up all kinds of fresh alternatives for the use of the past, yet the two cannot be easily harmonized.

One way around this difficulty is to pursue a two-track program. Much present instruction in history consists of "covering the material." Pages of text are assigned, the teacher lectures, asks questions or leads a discussion paralleling the assignment, and identifies "important points." After an interval of time—a few days or weeks—the student's ability to recall these points is checked.

The whole process is simple and routine. With a little effort, it can be reduced to essentials and accomplished efficiently and quickly. Conventional textbook-related work in history presents few intellectual problems that students cannot deal with on their own. Pages of the text can be assigned as homework, checked with a brief quiz at the beginning of class, and problem areas clarified or important points (familiar ideas) emphasized. The whole process need take no more than a few minutes. Information can also be presented effectively using outlines, summaries, worksheets, or computer programs.

With time available, many alternatives are possible. For example:

—Conventional history is much concerned with events that are related to patterns for the distribution of wealth and with public-sector decision making. The model suggests many other societal patterns which can be explored.

—Cultural premises are the mainsprings of human action, yet they are rarely even mentioned in history textbooks. They can be identified for the society being studied, their possible origins discussed, and their evolution traced.

—Historians make much use of the phrase *the dynamics of historical change,* but history textbooks provide no comprehensive, systematic models for the study of such change. The model provides such a framework. It can be applied to any society in any era.

—Underlying much historical writing are unexamined assumptions about human nature and about the workings of society. The model can be used to increase the student's awareness of these assumptions and of fallacies which may stem from them.

These are but a few of the possible alternatives for the study of the past suggested by the model. Any or all of them can be pursued. There is, however, one approach to the study of history that seems clearly superior. It is simple and direct. It is powerful and comprehensive. And it is applicable to any and every course in human history now included or ever likely to be included in the curriculum. The approach makes a single question the focus of all instruction: Who are these people we are trying to understand, and how did they become who they are? The question may seem vague and general—the kind of umbrella under which almost any activity is permissible. With the help of the model, however, the question can be answered with a precision and comprehensiveness far beyond that which is possible using conventional approaches to the study of the past.

In most history instruction, a simple but essential point is overlooked. A history must be a history of *something*—a machine, a person, an idea, a people. If an attempt is being made to describe how this "something" came to be, it is first necessary to establish as precisely as possible what it is. This is an absolutely critical first step, and conventional history instruction all but ignores it. The usual approach implies that by merely giving a people being studied a name and identifying a point in space and time they happen to occupy, something of substance has been created, the history of which can then be traced.

This will not do at all. It is with societies as it is with individuals. We do not know them until we know what is in their heads and how they are likely to act in various circumstances. *We cannot satisfactorily answer the question, How did these people become who they are? unless we first answer the question, Who are these people? And we can only answer this primary question with information about their cognitive system and patterns of action.*

In the study of American history, some teachers may think that this first step can be omitted, may assume that since most American history students are Americans, they already have an adequate answer to the question, Who are we? and can proceed directly to, How did we become who we are? That is not a correct assumption. Neither from formal education nor from life experience have most Americans acquired an understanding of their own cultural assumptions and patterns of action. They may know them at a level discussed earlier, the level at which most people knew about gravity before Newton, but that degree of knowing is far from adequate for academic purposes. Americans must begin their study of themselves at the same place they begin their study of any other society—with the question, Who are these people?

Not until students have answers to this question, not until they have some understanding of the conceptions of self, others, time, space, nature, causation, the good life, and other states of mind Americans share, and know at least the major ways in which these shared states of mind are manifested in distinctive patterns of action—not until then does it make sense to ask how the frontier experience, material abundance, selective immigration, or other factors fashioned this distinctive society.

We have very briefly described an approach to the history of human societies based on an attempt to answer the question, Who are these people, and how did they become who they are? Those who would defend traditional history instruction would no doubt insist that they are answering the same question. In a very general way, they may be right. But with so little time to teach, and so much to know if we are to survive, we cannot afford to pursue our educational objectives inefficiently.

A different approach to the study of the past may mean that students will have no time to hear or read about John Jay, the Battle of Lake Erie, or the XYZ Affair. But what of that? If our objectives for general education are the best we can devise, and if the work being done by students is in direct pursuit of those objectives, and if the traditional narrative is soon forgotten anyway, surely it is permissible to consign Jay and the Battle to the same storage area in which we usually keep Harmon Blennerhassett, Oliver Kelley, DeLima vs. Bidwell, and the Aroostock War. If we need them, we know where we can find them.

The Social Sciences

A consideration of the place of the social sciences in the traditional curriculum must begin with the recognition that the position they presently occupy is a relatively minor one. Although the really difficult individual and collective problems faced by humankind stem in one way or another from human interaction, at no educational level does the traditional curriculum require the systematic study of human behavior. In mathematics, language, natural science, and other fields students are moved year by year through more or less integrated, articulated, increasingly complex conceptual sequences. But in the study of *ourselves,* in the one area where ignorance and misunderstanding are the most costly and dangerous, it seems to be assumed that common sense and a smattering of history and geography provide students with all the understanding they need.

At the elementary level there is no systematic study of human behavior at all. In most secondary schools, a semester or year of introduction to two or three of the social sciences is available, but they are not always part of the required curriculum. Most postsecondary institutions offer a range of options in the social sciences, but for most students a random collection of introductory or survey courses will satisfy requirements for graduation. Little or no attempt is made to coordinate or integrate the courses either with each other or with other parts of the student's program of study.

American education's failure to meet the need for a formal study of humanness is recognized by a few educators, some of whom would increase the number of social science offerings. This is not a solution. There is, first of all, the inescapable fact that the curriculum is firmly established and the schedule relatively inflexible. Even if the social sciences met the need, the present courses of study are unlikely to be dropped to make room for multiyear programs in sociology, political science, economics, anthropology, and the other social sciences.

A second thrust for many years has been toward the creation of multidiscipline or interdiscipline social science courses. This is not a solution either, for there are fundamental problems within the social science disciplines themselves. The traditional social sciences are not products of a systematic attempt to create a comprehensive study of humankind. As Clyde Kluckhohn points out in *Mirror for Man:*

> To some people with neat academic minds the fields of knowledge dealing with human behavior are laid out like a series of formal gardens with walls

between . . . Some scholars indeed visualize these high, tight walls as actually existing and defend their frontiers against all poachers. But in actual practice some walls were never built or were so low they were easily leaped over by the more intrepid students; others have crumpled in the past decade or two. But, just because some students of man have believed in the reality of these walls, some of the most precious flowers in the gardens have failed to bear fruit. Moreover, some rich lands were never fenced in because ownership was in dispute. So they have been little cultivated, for the hardy scholar who ventured to follow his problem outside the walls of his own territory was punished by the suspicion and indignation of his more conservative colleagues. Hence, between and beyond the boundaries of the several social sciences, there is a vast no man's land.

In a discussion of the problem in *The Sociological Imagination,* C. Wright Mills makes a comment that curriculum designers, deans, and department heads should note: "It is more frequently in terms of textbooks than of *any other intellectual productions* that the . . . boundary making of 'fields' occur. It is difficult to imagine a less suitable locale" (emphasis added).

A third major difficulty in attempting to adapt the social sciences to the classroom is that, in their traditional form, they are not conceptually compatible. Superficial approaches to integration, such as team teaching or the study of a problem from the perspective of several disciplines, leave each discipline intact. The disciplines ask different questions, have different conceptual structures, and communicate with different words. The student who is exposed to political science and economics learns something about economics and political science, not some hybrid of the two.

Earlier I noted yet another reason why a unified, conceptually coherent social science appropriate for instruction is so elusive. Fragmentation of instruction stems from decades-long tendencies and traditions in the academic community. The pressure to specialize, to concentrate study on incredibly narrow concerns, has made strangers of many of those working within the same discipline. More often than not, particularly at the university level, those narrow studies become courses listed in the college catalog. Whether or not the information developed fits into a larger conceptual framework of use to the student is rarely even considered important. There are, in most of the social science disciplines, a few scholars who disregard the traditional boundaries, but their colleagues rarely pay them much attention.

Finally, the traditional social sciences resist adaptation to forms more appropriate for general education because they are institutionalized. Many teachers and most textbook authors are more concerned with teaching a particular social science discipline than in teaching about the phenomena the discipline was originally designed to study. Directing the student's attention to a subject called "economics" is not at all the same as directing his or her attention to economic activity, but this distinction is often overlooked. The fact that the whole world is a vast laboratory of human behavior waiting to be opened for study is generally disregarded in favor of sterile, two-dimensional textbooks which simply focus attention on the disciplines themselves.

It may not be possible to change the organization of the curriculum to make room for a unified approach to social science, may not be possible to move the academic community away from narrow specialization, may not be possible to shift the eyes of students out of their books and direct them to the real world, but it is certainly possible to structure present subjects and courses in unified ways. Social studies at the elementary level, history, economics, civics world geography, government, and sociology at the secondary level, and all the social sciences at the college level can, without major changes, become part of a single, integrated discipline. Most of the present content in all these offerings can continue to be used. Course titles can remain the same. Nothing now being done need be deleted. The task is to help students acquire a conceptual structure that organizes and relates these subjects, all of which deal in one way or another with humanness and therefore with the sociocultural systems which pattern humanness.

It is easy to be overwhelmed by the bulk and apparent randomness of the present social science curriculum. If, however, one concentrates on the fundamentals of the scientific approach to understanding human behavior, the task of creating an overarching conceptual structure becomes manageable. Just what is it we are trying to understand? Humanness. What does it mean to "understand?" It means knowing how that which is being studied is put together and how it usually works—its structure and functioning. With the structure and functioning of what phenomena are we concerned? Basic units of human organization—"natural human wholes," or "sociocultural systems." We have a model designed for that purpose.

What contribution can the model make to the study of, say, economics? It helps the beginning student understand what many professional economists do not yet adequately appreciate, that economics can only be understood in the context of the total system. Economic behavior is behavior inextricably linked to *all* the attributes of a particular sociocultural system—its demographics, environment, patterns of action and cultural premises, and the interaction of these components.

What, for example, could be more central to accurate economic prediction than the awareness that the number of people in a particular age group is declining, that a weather cycle is likely to mean years of decreasing rainfall in an area, that the number of single-parent households is increasing, or that ideas about what constitutes the good life are increasingly concerned with self-sufficiency?

That is the sort of information to which the model draws direct attention. Expanding the student's awareness of such factors will not make the student an economist (that is not the goal), but it will put the discipline in perspective, show very clearly its relationship to other disciplines, identify major variables in economic behavior, demonstrate that expansion of economic thought occurs through the exploration of relationships, and identify relevant factors involved in economic prediction. The student will have acquired a solid conceptual foundation for later specialization.

The economist Kenneth Boulding shares the view that an integrated, holistic approach to the study of economics is the proper approach to understanding. In *The Economics of Peace* he says the following: "Economic problems have no sharp edges; they shade off imperceptibly into politics, sociology, and ethics. Indeed, it is hardly an exaggeration to say that the ultimate answer to every economic problem lies in some other field." And in the Introduction to *A Reconstruction of Economics,* he makes this observation:

> I have been gradually coming under the conviction, disturbing for a professional theorist, that there is no such thing as economics—there is only social science applied to economic problems. Indeed, there may not even be such a thing as social science—there may only be general science applied to the problems of society.

There are social science teachers who could use the model to fashion a single social science instructional sequence appropriate for general education. However, few have sufficient latitude to adopt an approach so comprehensive. In most institutions teachers will find it necessary to stay within the bounds of existing course titles, catalog descriptions, and textbooks.

Within these bounds, in the design of isolated, general education social science courses, the model can serve two major functions. The first of these functions is to put the individual social science course in perspective. It hardly need be said that in the study of systems it is essential that the relationship of parts to wholes be clearly perceived. Unfortunately, most students enter their social science classes having little background in either social science or in the formal study of systems. Almost certainly they will never have studied sociocultural systems holistically. If they are to understand the role of a particular discipline in the search for the understanding of sociocultural wholes, they will need a conceptual model of those wholes.

The second major use of the model in the study of the traditional social sciences is as a source of conceptual relationships to be investigated. Instruction in social science should result in the formulation of concepts, but if the concepts are not used as tools in the exploration of relationships, the student will have learned little but a glossary of terms.

Suppose, for example, that in an introductory economics course the concept of scarcity has been presented. Does the ability to recognize a correct definition of the word on a multiple choice examination indicate understanding of the concept? Of course not. Does the ability to use the word correctly in a sentence demonstrate that it is understood in any useful way? Again, the answer is that it does not. Understanding is demonstrated by the ability to put a concept to work, to use it to answer questions which expand understanding.

What sort of questions? First, a basic one: How is scarcity related to choice? Then, those which touch on life as it is lived and which make apparent the significance of economic matters in the structure and functioning of sociocultural systems: What states of mind underlie and what patterns of action operationalize the relationships between scarcity and choice? And more specifically: How is scarcity related to patterns for work? For ownership? For decision making? To conceptions about the self? About the good life? Significant others? The supernatural?

Add to the concept of scarcity the three companion concepts of abundance, of transition from scarcity to abundance, and of transition from abundance to scarcity. Juxtapose each concept with each component of the model and ask, How are they related? The richness of the procedure, its power to expand and evaluate understanding, should be apparent.

What can be done with the concept of scarcity can be done with any social science concept, and what the model can do for economics it can do for political science, demography, sociology, cultural anthropology, archeology, social psychology, international relations, area and ethnic studies, human geography, and every other social science and branch thereof.

In our drive to specialize, we have directed attention to so many trees that the students cannot see the forest—the relatively simple fact that all meaningful human behavior occurs in the context of a particular sociocultural system and can only be understood within that context. That some of those systems are large, some small, some simple, some complex, some briefly lived, some long-lived, some contemporary, some ancient, some primitive makes no particular difference. A good model for the study of sociocultural systems can serve equally well as an aid in the study of a civilization, a corporation, a political bureaucracy, an Indian tribe, a religious cult, a family, a school class, an ethnic group, a neighborhood, a utopian dream, or even aliens from another planet.

The model outlines a social science that encompasses all the content of the traditional social sciences and much also that is at the present time

neglected. It provides a conceptual structure for scientific study that is intellectually manageable by average students of at least the upper-elementary level,
yet is complex enough to challenge the adult mind. It is dynamic, for it generates
the hypotheses which lead to its own elaboration and expansion. It provides
a conceptual base appropriate for the specializations of existing and yet-to-
be-developed social sciences. It establishes concrete criteria for content selection, and equips the student with a conceptual structure that integrates the
social sciences and relates them to the rest of the general studies curriculum.

The Humanities

Academic disciplines are supported by arguments which attempt to justify
their inclusion in the curriculum. These arguments are usually in the form of
statements of goals or educational objectives.

Of all the traditional areas of study, none has statements of instructional
objectives more abstract and lofty than those devised by the supporters of the
humanities. Prefatory material in humanities textbooks is likely to maintain,
for example, that studies of the humanities will increase human potential,
provide a basis for the formulation of a philosophy of life, enhance one's
self-awareness, be a source of insight into humanness, and contribute to the
development of perceptual and imaginative skills needed to understand
experience.

Those are admirable objectives. However, when one moves from the
preface to the body of most humanities textbooks, the objectives tend to
slip out of sight. If routine course content relates at all to the formal statements
of objectives, it does so in such a subtle fashion that the two probably will
not actually meet in the mind of the average student. The best-selling
textbooks in the field concern themselves primarily with "styles," "movements,"
"schools," and "periods" of artistic production. Exposition and graphics
describe and interpret works which, using various criteria, are perceived
as belonging together. The mechanics of getting from course content to
the kind of instructional objectives found in the textbook introductions is left
to the student.

But humanities instruction is both that which it actually is in working
classrooms, and that which those who fashion the soaring language of
humanities textbook introductions like to believe that it is. In the pursuit
of abstract objectives (objectives considered by some to be soft or fuzzy-
headed because they cannot be measured) the model provides specific
and concrete direction. These kinds of humanities objectives generally
reflect the view that humanness is acquired and that each individual grows
into it gradually as experience is evaluated and responses to certain questions

are fashioned, questions such as the following: Who am I? What would it be like to be someone else? What does it mean to be human? How can I make sense out of the world? How can I be free? What are my responsibilities? How am I related to others? To nature? To time? Why do I perceive this as ugly and that as beautiful?

The model, particularly that part having to do with cultural premises, provides students with some very direct help with these questions. It says to them that they are products of a particular cultural system, an entity that predisposes them to act and think in certain ways and to feel that these ways of acting and thinking are generally superior, or at least preferable, to other ways of thinking and acting. It tells them that the sociocultural system of which they are a part has invented certain answers to questions about the nature of the self, of existence and freedom, and about one's "proper" relationship to nature, time, and space. It tells them that they will tend to accept without question most of the premises of their native society, because these premises are so deeply imbedded in their cognitive system and so reinforced by language and patterns of action that they have difficulty even imagining alternatives. In short, the first contribution of the model to the attainment of the more abstract humanities instructional objectives is that it helps students see how personal experience, focused by and filtered through the peculiar lens of the society within which they have grown up, has shaped them.

Use of the model can lead directly to the achievement of the highest level of humanities objectives. Ordinarily, however, these objectives are assumed to be attained indirectly, as the student engages in the day-to-day task of attempting to understand, organize, and interpret the art, architecture, music, literature, and other creative effort of different peoples and eras. For this task also the model provides a comprehensive conceptual framework. It establishes the elementary and important fact that creativity can only be understood from "inside," in terms established by the sociocultural system of which the creator is or was a member. What is written or painted or designed means only what those within a sociocultural system intend it to mean. A dance is not just a dance. It is whatever those who devise it, perform it, or watch it make of it. The very same movement may, in the context of one society, be an act of worship, while in another it may have sexual meaning. In yet another society the movement may be designed to manipulate the spirit world. There is no way to know what is meant simply by looking at the thing created, nor is there any way for outsiders to see it in just the way it is seen by those within the originating culture. The most the outsider can do is speculate about its meaning, and the only valid approach to that is to try to grasp the totality of the sociocultural system of which the creation is a part.

The model also helps the student understand that dance, music, literature, sculpture, painting, architecture, language, village design, philosophical system, and everything else within a particular society will tend to be more or less consistent, for all will be products of the basic cultural premises of that system. The Indian musical composition, for example, moving along without pause, without climax, with little change in tempo or dynamics, is perfectly in tune with fundamental cultural premises of Indian society.

The model facilitates the study of those who are members of other sociocultural systems, individuals very likely to have different assumptions about life, self, time, causation, and so forth. It points out that many of these alien patterns and premises are not just different but may also be interesting, beautiful, complex, logical, valid, and useful. As this happens, awareness of differences clarifies thinking about one's own patterns of action and cultural assumptions and opens up myriad possibilities for alternative action. One can begin to appreciate the exciting and challenging fact that there are endless ways of being human, and that some of the alternatives may present more realistic or more satisfying responses to the world than those responses one calls one's own. When this happens, freedom expands and other humanities objectives begin to be realized. Self-awareness is heightened and perception of the range of human potential is broadened.

For the teacher designing or revising a humanities course, all previous discussion concerning the role of the model is applicable. Its primary value lies in its ability to put content in perspective. Separated from their cultural context, artistic productions have little meaning. The model is a relatively simple device for helping students see the wholes of which individual creations are projections. Its use will of course require class time that would previously have been used to "cover the material," but the benefits surely far exceed the costs.

Beyond the model's use as a device to put humanities content in perspective, the cultural premises component is particularly helpful as a conceptual organizer for the humanities. Every society's productions reflect their cognitive system—their conceptions of the nature of self, others, humanness, time, and so forth. Adoption of a formal category system for these concepts, a system that is carried from society to society and from era to era as an analytical tool, will do much to simplify the student's task.

In fact, a good argument could be assembled for making a category system for the study of cultural premises the primary organizer of humanities data. In such an approach, instead of simply surveying each style or era in turn, instruction would begin by establishing a major element of the student's cognitive system, exploring its manifestation in the student's native culture, then moving on to manifestations of that same element as it is embodied in the artistic productions of other cultures.

For the teacher who is willing to think freshly about the content and organization of humanities instruction, the model suggests many other possibilities—alternatives to present practice which both allow the highest-order, most-general humanities objectives to be pursued in systematic, concrete fashion, and which place the traditional content in contexts which make it more manageable, memorable, and useful.

Language

Every academic discipline can be strengthened by clarifying its cultural base and fitting its conceptual structure within the largest possible knowledge framework. In the study of language, however, this process is hardly necessary. The structure of a language and the culture of its native speakers are so tightly interwoven that they cannot be separated. Neither can exist without the other. Every insight into a language opens a window on the culture of which it is a part; every insight into the culture opens a window on the language. We may not choose to look through those windows, or we may not yet be perceptive enough to interpret what we see, but the windows are there.

The potential contribution of a study of sociocultural systems to increased understanding of language is great. Unfortunately, not much of that potential is likely soon to be realized. A survey of present classroom practice makes the reason apparent: many of those responsible for the day-to-day decisions about language study have only a narrow interest in language. It follows then that if there is little interest in understanding language, there is little need for tools to expand understanding.

What is the primary interest of many teachers of language? It is easily summarized. They want their students to learn to speak, read, and write their own or another language "correctly." To that end, spelling is tested, vocabulary exercises are assigned, reading is practiced, speeches are made, essays are written, and grammar is studied. In each activity the teacher's role is much the same—to point out deviations from whatever the teacher considers correct. Routine assignments often indicate little interest in language itself—in language as a peculiar phenomenon, language as a complex puzzle, language as a source of insight into self, language as a key to how the mind works, language as a map to guide the study of familiar and unfamiliar societies.

Little wonder, then, that the study of sociocultural systems may seem unrelated to the study of language. If language education is perceived primarily as a matter of having students "rehearse the language until they get it right," if they are merely learning language and not at the same time learning about the phenomenon of language, there is no need for conceptual tools designed to increase understanding.

Of these two emphases—learning a language and understanding language—the latter ought surely to occupy a place equal to the former in the general education curriculum. What could be more central to general education than a study of that without which humanness is impossible? We need to ask the larger questions about language, questions to which we tend to think we already have answers. What is language? What does it do? How does it do what it does? That we humans make so little effort to deepen our understanding of that which sets us so apart from all else is a question that students in a language class in general education ought to think about. Here are others:

—What is a "word"? How many kinds are there?. What is a "sentence"? What does it mean to "know" a language? What does "correct language" mean? Who decides? Upon what basis? What are the uses of answers to these questions?

—Every language exists in many styles and substyles—a style for speaking with close friends, for example, and within this style, variations dependent upon age, sex, and situation. There are styles related to status, styles for public address, styles for speaking to one's self, styles for solemn occasions, styles for talking to God or the gods, styles for telling secrets, and many, many others. How many such styles can be identified? How do they differ? Why? Under what circumstances is each employed? What are the consequences of the use of a wrong style? How early in life is there an awareness and use of differing styles? Of what value are answers to these questions?

—Within the same language, subtle differences in speech can mean the difference between acceptance and rejection, success and failure. What are these differences? Where are they found? What purposes do they serve? Why are such differences often deliberately maintained or even emphasized in the face of apparently negative consequences? Of what use are answers to these questions?

—Does a language bias its users' perceptions of experience, encouraging, facilitating, or even requiring certain ways of thinking and discouraging, making difficult, or impossible other ways of thinking? If so, which ways of thinking? Are some languages better than others? More suitable for some purposes or in some situations than other languages? What purposes or situations?

—Why do languages change? What problems does language change create? Solve? Are there patterns in or directions to the changes? Does language make social change more or less difficult? Why? Are changes in language resisted? If so, by whom? When? How? Why?

—What problems and benefits stem from language differences? Dialect differences? Are attitudes toward language variations related to attitudes toward those who use the variations? If so, how? Why do those who speak two languages sometimes have feelings of language inadequacy, while those who speak only one language do not?

To teachers of language who have dedicated their professional lives to correcting student errors, other language-related activity may be unacceptable. The move from language mechanic to language scientist, from language "insider" to "outsider," from language as something to tell about to language as something to ask about may seem a distant journey. Many will have no wish to make that journey. They will see it as trivial or pointless, or as inappropriate for the students they teach, or as a diversion from the important task of preparing for standardized tests, or as not possible because the textbooks do not point the way, or as a matter to be left to the experts. In any case, many teachers will have little interest in a map to guide their own or the students' exploration of the relationships between language and culture.

I am not advocating that emphasis on language understanding be at the expense of language facility. Students must function in a world in which the degree of skill in the use of language has very real and important consequences. They need all the help they can get in learning to communicate more effectively. But facility in our own or another language is far less than an adequate objective of language study in general education. We need to put the whole of language in perspective, need to get outside and above it, from which vantage point we can control it rather than it us. In that effort, a model for the study of sociocultural systems is a very valuable tool.

The Natural Sciences

Black holes in space. Music. The nature of smell. Bacteria which thrive on the sea floor at temperatures and pressures far greater than those in a laboratory autoclave. The incredibly complex collective behavior of certain insects . . .

To mysteries such as these there is no end. Any randomly chosen bit of the universe seems to enclose puzzles beyond count, and the pursuit of understanding increases rather than diminishes their number. Around such mysteries a never-ending course of study can be fashioned, a study that can begin in infancy and extend through all the years of life.

Such a study belongs in the schools. An adequate rationale for it is simply that there *are* mysteries. We are naturally curious, and exploring that about which we are curious is human and fulfilling. It is also the foundation of basic research, the unexpected results of which generally prove beneficial to humankind. School science should have no boundaries. Anything and everything is potentially exciting and important.

There are, however, certain aspects of the natural world which it is imperative to understand not simply because they are challenging or fun, but because the nature and quality of our lives, and sometimes life itself, depend upon understanding. We can afford a degree of ignorance about, say, optical phenomena or the composition of the rings of Saturn. We can*not* afford to be ignorant about any aspect of the physical world that is integrally linked to the well-being of humankind. It is this concern that establishes the boundaries of a natural science appropriate for general education. To state it precisely: A natural science for general education should explore those parts and aspects of the physical world which affect or have the potential for affecting the structure or functioning of sociocultural systems.

The focus of such a science is sharp, but its scope is by no means narrow. Anything that alters or is likely to alter the characteristics of a society's demographics or environment, thereby exerting pressure on its important patterns of action or cognitive system, needs to be identified and monitored, and the implications or those alternatives understood. Biological, technological, physiological, and environmental changes should be continuously observed and analyzed. A region's water table dropping a centimeter a year or taking ever longer to recover, a growing season decreasing by a few days each century, a gradual change in the composition of the atmosphere, an annual expansion of a desert by a hundred meters or so, the steady depletion of a nonrenewable resource, the gradual appearance or disappearance of a particular organism in the ocean—these are the kinds of changes which, unnoticed, can cause human societies to shudder, bend or disintegrate, with those whose lives are altered or ended never knowing the sources of their trauma.

A science that grows out of an attempt to identify and monitor these kinds of changes and to determine their actual and potential impact on sociocultural systems should be part of an integrated general education curriculum.

Mathematics

Making change, computing gas mileage, balancing the checkbook, figuring how much kitchen tile is needed—all sorts of daily, mundane activities require the use of mathematics. It is an indispensable tool, one that the schools must help every student acquire.

The value and frequency of use of simple mathematical concepts and skills, however, may lead to some questionable assumptions about the place of mathematics in the curriculum. Because some mathematics is obviously a good thing, it does not necessarily follow that, for purposes of general education, more of the same mathematics is better. Certainly students who have mathematical ability should be helped to move as far and as fast as possible, but that is no less than should be done for students who can sing, dance, write computer programs, build beautiful tables, or generate promising hypotheses about the cause of a disease. The general education component of the curriculum should not be shaped by considerations of the potential of one segment of the student population.

In defense of mathematical study, the usual argument is that it contributes to "mental discipline" or that it develops "logical processes." For purposes of general education, these are not very strong arguments. Mathematical study may have that potential, but the mechanical nature of much instruction makes such benefits unlikely to be realized in the average classroom. Even if it can be proven that mathematics instruction does indeed develop transferable cognitive skills, with so little instructional time available it would seem to make more sense to develop those skills in contexts which do not require transfer but which are immediately useful.

Mathematics—a great deal of it—belongs in the curriculum. But for general education, once students have acquired the simple concepts and skills that daily routine requires, the mathematics needed is a mathematics that helps make sense of experience. What important characteristics of system population can be quantified, what are the numbers, and how are the numbers changing? What is happening to the environment—to wealth, to climate, to resources, to tools? Which patterns of action are followed by how many, and how are the patterns changing? What segments of the population believe what? How strongly?

Answers to questions such as these help us put our situations in perspective and increase our control over our fates. Mathematics needs to be taken out into the real world—not simply out to concerns about balancing checkbooks and making change, but to all dimensions of reality. There is much in daily experience that, in the absence of concepts for dealing with its quantitative aspects, eludes understanding. To see clearly the shape of the present, the curves of history, the probable and possible contours of the future, mathematical ideas are essential. What students need is not game playing with numbers, but conceptual tools for making sense of experience. We need to use mathematics, daily, need to close the books and begin to take the measure of ourselves and the world around us. We need to find out what is happening to us, when, where, and with what intensity and frequency. To that end mathematics is a major means. To simply play with it because it is there, or because the puzzles it presents are interesting or challenging, is irresponsible.

Social Problems

Social problems courses, and the many courses which deal with one or more specific problems, might seem to provide satisfactory ways to keep instruction in touch with reality and to encourage the use of many disciplines. Perhaps the approach has that potential, but in actual practice the potential is seldom realized.

The difficulty begins with the concept of 'problem'. Although it is possible to devise a rather precise definition of the term, the task of defining is not often undertaken and the complexity is rarely appreciated. There is instead an assumption that problems are more or less self-evident and that all that is necessary for instruction to begin is that particular ones be chosen for study. Air or water pollution, law and order, war, poverty, the economy, prejudice, and energy are the sort of "problems" often studied.

Ordinarily a problem has not been determined to be a problem by the application of objective criteria. It is simply a condition or situation that has received media attention. Although it is likely that all the problems studied in social problems courses really are problems (at least to someone), to assume that public awareness and media notice will somehow always focus on the important questions and the relevant aspects of those questions is naive. The amount of public attention a situation receives is rarely proportional to the degree of threat it poses. Many factors go into the making of the perception of the problem, and many of those factors have little to do with its intensity or the situation's potentially negative impact on individuals or society.

Even if the most important problems *were* those identified by the media and public opinion, traditional approaches to their study would have inherent and serious weaknesses. One of those weaknesses stems from the inevitable lag between the perception and the acceptance of a situation or condition as a problem, and the appearance of the matter in the classroom as a subject of study. If the objective of problems study is ultimately to help students cope with problems, then what they and society need is not a forum for discussing situations which are almost always in a stage of development beyond what is being discussed. What is needed is a conceptual structure and skills which allow problems to be anticipated before they have created sufficient chaos to become a topic of general discussion. Social problems, like physical illnesses, are easier to prevent than to cure. And they are easier to cope with when detected early than when discovered late.

A related difficulty that almost always attends the study of contemporary problems is that, by the time issues reach the classroom, they have become emotionally charged. Lively discussions and argument may be possible, but it is doubtful that much of intellectual value really takes place. Most students probably leave a heated classroom discussion holding even more tightly to whatever positions they originally held. When study focuses on problems yet to come, however, there is much less likelihood that the whole effort will seem to be an empty exercise. Students are perfectly aware that by the time a problem or issue reaches the classroom they have little or no ability to influence the situation. Knowing that, classwork related to existing problems is likely to seem a pointless game.

The model provides a means for coming at traditional social problems courses in a more intellectually demanding, useful, and less emotionally charged fashion. It also makes clear that 'problem' is a narrower concept than the student originally may have supposed. Problems are defined by values. In one sociocultural system, hunger may be a problem. In another, the same degree of hunger may be ignored or may be seen as an opportunity for spiritual growth. Problems are whatever the people involved consider to be problems. They occur in the context of sociocultural systems and should be evaluated primarily in terms of those systems.

Finally, the model provides a means for studying problems and potential problems at a time in their evolution when they may still be responsive to positive action. By identifying the major elements of the system being studied and the nature and direction of changes within and between those elements, it is possible to come to some useful conclusions about changes which can be anticipated and problems which may be created or exacerbated by those changes. It makes it possible to see relationships between problems and to see why "solutions" almost always create new problems. Finally, the model provides a means for defining situations more objectively and establishing potential troublesomeness on the basis of impact on the stability and adaptability of the system.

Futures

Social change creates a different world for each new generation. It is ironic, then, that the study of futures has so little place in the curriculum. However, a few schools do offer courses, and if the curriculum must be fragmented, arguments for including a study of futures as one of the fragments are persuasive.

Although it is impossible to predict even tomorrow's events with certainty, assumptions about the future which amount to prediction are made constantly. In fact, to make reasonably valid decisions in the present, there is no alternative to making assumptions about the future. Deciding how much and what kind of education to seek, choosing an occupational field, or even thinking about how and when to spend a paycheck requires assumptions that the future will or will not bring changes in levels of security or wealth, that one's job will or will not continue, that the cost of fuel will stay the same or go up or down. Routine decisions based on assumptions about the future are made constantly— that crime, neighborliness, the price of housing, or the percentage of income allotted to taxes will increase, decrease, or remain static. The future cannot be predicted, but nearly everyone projects probable and possible futures and acts on the basis of those projections.

Futures courses can help students approach more systematically the task of speculating about the future of those sociocultural systems of significance to them. These courses can provide skills and techniques for making necessary projections more reliable. They can help trace the implications and ramifications of present decisions and the various futures those decisions could create. Finally, futures study can help people devise strategies which may be useful in attempts to avoid or minimize problems and stresses.

In these activities, the model functions in much the same way as it does when used to study history or an unfamiliar society. At the most elementary level, it provides a checklist of specifically what it is about a particular sociocultural system that may change—those aspects of demographics, environment, patterns of action, and cultural premises, changes in which will make the future unlike the present. The model identifies the elements and points to the systemic interactions which will create the specific future that will emerge. And it provides a summary of the present against which various probable and possible futures can be juxtaposed to identify potential sources of stress and conflict.

The future cannot be predicted, but it can be said with certainty that it will be unlike the present, and that the significant changes will be those which alter sociocultural systems. Aspects of reality which, when they change, cause other things to change can be identified. It is also possible to identify the general nature of the personal and institutional stresses which change will bring, so that a variety of strategies for coping with those stresses can be divised.

Every improvement in a society's ability to trace the outlines of possible and probable futures contributes directly to the likelihood of its members being able to fashion a preferable future. On any list of general education objectives, helping students gain a measure of control over the future ought to rank high.

Area Studies

The various approaches to the description and explanation of human affairs which are used in area studies courses are usually an improvement over traditional, discipline-bound approaches. There are, however, inadequacies in the general concept of area studies.

Problems begin with the term itself, for *area studies* suggests that areas have inherent characteristics or an internal structure that can organize, systematize, or simplify study. They do not. Although, like the concept of time, the concept of space is often used to organize the study of humankind, its usefulness is overrated. Mere existence in a particular point in space explains little of value. In fact, it can get the student off on a wrong foot by implying that areas are meaningful, manageable units of study. Characteristics of the physical world are of course important in shaping human affairs, but they are not, as is implied by the phrase *area studies,* important enough to be perceived as a primary consideration.

A second problem with the concept of area studies is the implication that boundaries are important, that what happens within an area relates primarily and most importantly to that area. As events daily demonstrate, however, that is by no means the case. Actions in remote parts of the world can (and often do) trigger reactions far beyond an area's boundaries.

If it is contemporary human affairs about which understanding is sought, it is not areas but sociocultural systems which must be the focus of study. Everyday experience confirms it. There are thousands of places on the surface of the earth where two or more groups occupy the same geographic area while differing fundamentally from each other. In fact, it is possible for several societies to occupy the same tightly defined area continuously and yet have almost no contact with each other. The Kluckhohns demonstrated the relative neutrality of area characteristics years ago in their study of a location in New Mexico. On the same soil, in the same climate, on the same terrain, within the same political boundary, five different sociocultural systems pursued vastly different ways of life.

The term *area studies* may suggest the problems noted; however, the problems rarely materialize. Area studies tend to be open-ended, and the eclectic approach that characterizes most instruction usually insures considerable flexibility. Adapting the model for use in area studies simply requires that it be adopted and that it be applied within an area to specific, relatively coherent social or cultural entities.

Global Education

In recent years the term *global education* has gained currency, and national, state, and local educational organizations have gone on record in support of the concept. The objectives are admirable. According to the literature, the aims are to study nations, cultures, and peoples, with emphasis on how these elements are interconnected, how the relationships change, and with what individuals should be concerned in a world of global interdependence. The U. S. Commissioner of Education's Task Force on Global Education concluded that "global perspectives must be grounded broadly in the various disciplines— the natural sciences, the humanities, and the social sciences—and must also draw upon the fresh analysis of systems and other concepts."

Unfortunately, given the general unresponsiveness of the institution of education to new programs, it is not likely that these sweeping objectives will actually be translated into a great number and variety of instructional activities

Special Classes

FOREIGN STUDENTS. In recent years the relative ease of travel and changes in the distribution of wealth have resulted in considerable increases in the number of students from other cultures enrolled in American schools and universities. The problems are about what one would expect—difficulties with the language, teacher use of explanatory allusions not understood by those reared elsewhere, content inappropriate for or inapplicable to life in other societies, ethnocentric biases in instruction and instructional materials, and instructional objectives framed without consideration for nontraditional students. Problems are sometimes less marked in technical fields; it is in general education that the greatest difficulties arise, the most student potential is wasted, and the richest opportunities for both foreign and native students are left unexplored and unexploited.

Given a reasonable degree of teacher flexibility, the model can help with all these problems. Used as a basis for a special class or incorporated into traditional general education courses, the model becomes a means to the achievement of the full range of the objectives already identified. It can tailor the general education program to the individual student, making that program as valid and useful for the foreign student who returns home as it is for American students here. It provides a comprehensive conceptual structure the foreign student can use to better understand the dominant American society and the various subcultures with which he or she may have contact. It can make the foreign student a real classroom asset, for the model can become a vehicle for comparative cultural study, with both foreign and native students serving as sources of systematically organized information in classroom explorations of each other's societies, explorations which enlighten and broaden both those who ask and those who answer questions.

Alfred North Whitehead once observed, "The second-handedness of the learned world is the secret of its mediocrity." The presence of both American and foreign students in the same classroom presents unparalleled opportunities for first-hand experience. What is necessary to take advantage of the opportunities this contact presents for intellectual and emotional growth is a reasonably culturally-neutral guide to channel communication and structure understanding. The model serves that purpose.

FOREIGN TRAVEL. Students who travel abroad to observe unfamiliar contemporary societies or to see the preserved artifacts of earlier societies face the same conceptual problems as the student of history, the new employee in the corporation, the archeologist, the cultural anthropologist, or the new resident in town. They are confronted with tremendous amounts of raw data—

Special Classes

FOREIGN STUDENTS. In recent years the relative ease of travel and changes in the distribution of wealth have resulted in considerable increases in the number of students from other cultures enrolled in American schools and universities. The problems are about what one would expect—difficulties with the language, teacher use of explanatory allusions not understood by those reared elsewhere, content inappropriate for or inapplicable to life in other societies, ethnocentric biases in instruction and instructional materials, and instructional objectives framed without consideration for nontraditional students. Problems are sometimes less marked in technical fields; it is in general education that the greatest difficulties arise, the most student potential is wasted, and the richest opportunities for both foreign and native students are left unexplored and unexploited.

Given a reasonable degree of teacher flexibility, the model can help with all these problems. Used as a basis for a special class or incorporated into traditional general education courses, the model becomes a means to the achievement of the full range of the objectives already identified. It can tailor the general education program to the individual student, making that program as valid and useful for the foreign student who returns home as it is for American students here. It provides a comprehensive conceptual structure the foreign student can use to better understand the dominant American society and the various subcultures with which he or she may have contact. It can make the foreign student a real classroom asset, for the model can become a vehicle for comparative cultural study, with both foreign and native students serving as sources of systematically organized information in classroom explorations of each other's societies, explorations which enlighten and broaden both those who ask and those who answer questions.

Alfred North Whitehead once observed, "The second-handedness of the learned world is the secret of its mediocrity." The presence of both American and foreign students in the same classroom presents unparalleled opportunities for first-hand experience. What is necessary to take advantage of the opportunities this contact presents for intellectual and emotional growth is a reasonably culturally-neutral guide to channel communication and structure understanding. The model serves that purpose.

FOREIGN TRAVEL. Students who travel abroad to observe unfamiliar contemporary societies or to see the preserved artifacts of earlier societies face the same conceptual problems as the student of history, the new employee in the corporation, the archeologist, the cultural anthropologist, or the new resident in town. They are confronted with tremendous amounts of raw data—

unfamiliar stimuli which must be sorted out, assigned meaning, given priority, related, and integrated to form an understandable picture of a social entity. The fundamental similarity of this task to those previously discussed should make apparent the applicability and usefulness of the model in travel abroad. Like the childhood puzzle in which a picture begins to emerge as numbered dots are connected with lines, the outlines of unfamiliar societies begin to emerge as the information called for by the model is identified. The model does not provide the student with a map of an unfamiliar culture, but it does provide guidelines useful in constructing one. It also reminds the student that much that is novel or exotic may be of little or no significance in the attempt to understand an unfamiliar society.

INSTITUTIONAL ORIENTATION. I suggested in chapter 1 that a major weakness in the traditional curriculum is its failure to help the student understand those institutions which structure daily action, institutions which determine in large measure our well-being, happiness, and success. We do not ordinarily step outside our religious, economic, political, social, and educational organizations far enough to be able to see them with the critical and objective eye that distance provides. We tend, for example, to view our schools and universities merely as sources of what might be called "standard services." How these institutions work, we feel, is of little interest or consequence as long as services continue to be provided. They are sort of educational vending machines. Year after year they stand in the same locations, offering the same choices, requiring payment and perhaps a routine shake or kick before delivering the standard credit. We are vaguely aware that someone loads the machine, that some kind of mechanisms respond to the coins or kick and thereupon transport the fare to the aperture. However, preoccupied by the nature of the fare, the machine itself is taken for granted and largely ignored.

This ought not to be. The appropriateness of the choices the machine provides, the general nature of the mechanisms it contains, the payments it exacts and the reasons for them, and the length of the interval between loading and sale are themselves part of the transaction. They are something to be understood, and the customer, the machine, and those in charge of the machine will be better off if they *are* understood.

In vending machines, wear and obsolescence are natural and inevitable. They are constantly being rebuilt and redesigned. In human institutions, increasing program inefficiency and obsolescence are equally natural and inevitable. And, just as it is desirable that in the redesign of vending machines the customers, engineers, designers, service personnel, repairers, and others contribute to its improvement, so it is that our schools, legislatures, courts, religious groups, and other institutions can be improved by the suggestions of all those who affect and are affected by them.

Before that can happen, however, the workings of the machine as it is must be exposed. Inspection plates, covers, and housings must be removed (usually over the protests of those who have come to feel that the machines are their exclusive property and that therefore their nature and functioning are no one else's business). When the workings are open to view and study, then some kind of guide or handbook is needed. In an orientation to the educational "machines" we have created, the model can serve that purpose. Although other conceptual schemes for analyzing the structure and functioning of an institution are available, two arguments favor use of the model.

First, if the model is already being used in one or more of the required general education courses, applying it in a different dimension of reality reinforces and strengthens the concepts it teaches. Humanities, language, history, the social sciences, "institutional orientaton," and other courses using the model become mutually supportive. Second, the model is a better guide than the catalogs, public relations brochures, media releases, organizational charts, and other communications which usually emerge from administrative suites as explanations of how the institution is structured and how it functions. Some discomfort may result if students begin to ask questions about, say, the shape of classrooms in the new wing (environment), the assumptions of those responsible for their shape (cultural premises), and the mechanisms (patterns of action) whereby those assumptions were translated into a final design, but the interests of students, the institution, and the larger society will in the long run be served.

Discussion of the implications of the relative size and decor of the offices of various institutional employees, of budget items and the priorities they reflect, of patterns for making decisions, indeed of all aspects of the model as they apply to the institution, can, if properly focused, provide an orientation worthy of the name. Students need to know the location of the library and locker rooms. They need to be acquainted with campus routine. But those kinds of benefits pale beside those which a genuine orientation course could provide. Students could learn first-hand how one human institution *really* works, and they in turn could help that institution and others to which they belong meet their most important objectives—sustained effectiveness through self-renewal.

Limitations of the Model

The constant repetition of the phrase *The Model can . . .* has almost certainly become tiresome. I hope it is clear, however, that *it is not the attributes of the model but the ubiquitousness of what it represents* that makes it so broadly applicable. Other models of sociocultural systems can demonstrate with equal clarity the unfortunate arbitrariness and awkwardness of the boundaries we have created between fields of knowledge. They can also demonstrate my contention that the firmer one's grasp of the concept of culture, the easier it is to see why and how it pulls the random bits of the present curriculum together, fills the empty spaces between them, and molds them into a true curricular system.

Any number of elementary models can be used to introduce the concept of sociocultural system and to guide instruction related to it. The one I have described, however, based on years of experimentation, has proved to be a practical, workable tool. Thousands of students of differing age, ability, nationality, cultural heritage, and academic level have used it. It has guided the study of neighborhoods, corporations, nations, ethnic groups, ancient civilizations, utopian and fictional societies, religious movements, city-states, tribes, ships' crews, schools, military installations, athletic teams, youth gangs, revolutionaries, and other human systems. It has been used to structure comparative studies of rural and urban subcultures, to trace differences between "town and gown," to contrast those living on "opposite sides of the railroad track," to clarify conflicts and misunderstanding between various groups, and as a basis for counseling marriage partners of differing cultural background.

As with all models, however, this one creates for its users a potentially serious problem. Although new models of reality liberate and expand our thinking, they also soon begin to have negative effects. What begins as *a* way of representing reality in order to make it intellectually manageable tends increasingly to become *the* way of viewing reality. Instead of checking our model against reality to see how it should be changed to make it more accurate and useful, we tend to accept only information that fits with or reinforces the model we have come to find so comfortable and useful. The longer we use a particular model, the more difficult it generally becomes to change it.

We can try to build in obstacles to this tendency. To begin with, the fact that the use of the model is conscious and deliberate reminds us that it is merely a model and that it should not be allowed to structure thinking too rigidly. Second, the categories of the model are very general and allow considerable latitude for interpretation and application. Finally, if ever the significance and centrality of the study of sociocultural systems is appreciated, it is likely that alternative models and variations on those models will be constantly appearing. The more models there are, the less likely is it that any one of them will become rigidly institutionalized. The teacher can also contribute to flexibility by making it clear that a model is merely a starting point, a temporary structure to be constantly torn apart and rebuilt as experience and analysis suggest ever-more-useful forms. Model evolution can also be encouraged by presenting aspects of reality which do not fit comfortably into the model being used and challenging students to reconcile the two.

Incidentally, activities such as this can serve another valuable purpose. They can demonstrate that the phenomena related to humanity are inherently complex and challenging and worthy of the best effort of the best students. It is ironic that social studies, the elementary- and secondary-level school subject that by title would seem to come nearest to being a study of the complexity of humankind, is regularly ranked by students as the least-challenging area of study. As a consequence, many students who might eventually be able to contribute much to our understanding of ourselves and others turn for intellectual stimulation to mathematics and natural science.

It is not possible to devise a model for the study of sociocultural systems that will adequately interpret reality for every student in every situation. But almost any model consciously and deliberately fashioned will at least begin to meet what is surely the most critical educational need we face.

Appendix A. Notes on Teaching

I began playing with models for teaching about the concept of culture about twenty-five years ago. Since then, I've worked with students at every level from elementary school through the university, students representing the range of abilities, interests, and inclinations found in most public schools and colleges. I've taught in a half-dozen different institutions in several different fields. I've administered, observed, consulted, supervised, coordinated, written articles, books, and computer programs for and about education. Nevertheless, I'm reluctant to generalize from experience. Individual differences in students, differences in ethnic and regional background, differences in teacher personality and philosophy, in level of maturity of academic discipline, in instructional materials, in administrative style and presence, in physical facilities, and much else convince me that I'm unlikely to be able to give usefully precise advice about how to teach. I'm most comfortable, therefore, in saying, "Here are some thoughts I've had and some approaches I've tried in my efforts to expand student understanding of sociocultural systems. Perhaps my comments will give you some useful ideas."

Preliminaries

I walk into my classes on the first day of school aware that my approach to teaching is idiosyncratic (as it is with all teachers). Since students will find my classes different, and since all of us may react to the unfamiliar with fear, anxiety, indignation, or apathy, I try to identify the peculiarities in my classroom behavior and to make both the idiosyncrasies and the students' possible reactions to them matters of thorough discussion. The relationship of student to teacher isn't ordinarily a casual one. If it takes a few hours to establish a good working relationship, I consider the time well spent. I don't feel compelled to confront students on the first day of class with a formidable chunk of that which we'll eventually be exploring. I'd rather visit together, finding out who they are, letting them know who I am, and discussing some of the assumptions we've brought with us, assumptions which might bear on the success (or lack of it) of our exploration.

Some of these assumptions have to do with the nature of the student-teacher relationship. If I find myself in a conventional classroom with conventional furniture conventionally arranged, after we've visited awhile, I may begin a discussion of our relationship by asking the students to think and talk about the implications of the environment in which we find ourselves. What does the furniture imply about their role? About their relationship to me? To each other? Where are the empty spaces, and what do they mean? Who "owns" the blackboard, and what of that? Are the height of the ceiling, the orientation of the furniture to the entrance area, the very fact that there is such a room at all, useful to us in our attempt to understand the assumptions about education we have probably absorbed from the society of which we are a part?

And when we have noted the messages which seem to be transmitted by this environment in which we find ourselves, we question the validity of those messages. The desk, the podium, the empty space, for example, imply teacher authority. What sort of authority? Based upon what assumptions? How valid *are* those assumptions? And so on.

Roles

One of the messages transmitted by the arrangement of the typical classroom is that the teacher is an expert on the subject at hand. Now there are a few matters on which I might be so considered, but in my view the "expert" role is of limited pedagogical use. I'm not interested in students leaving my class with a few hundred answers borrowed from me and soon to be forgotten. They don't need yesterday's or today's answers. They need tomorrow's answers, and I don't have them.

I'm much more interested in students leaving my class as *real* students—curious, probing, interested, self-propelled, alive. That seems more likely to happen if they perceive *me* as curious, probing, interested, self-propelled, alive—being, as much as I can be, the kind of student I want them to be. Obviously this doesn't mean that I adopt student mannerisms or that I fail to meet my responsibilities in matters of classroom routine. I simply want to model the kind of actions and attitudes which, if adopted, would allow my students to help themselves grow. Permanently.

As for my teacher role, what I need for that is not an answer to every question. I need to have a general grasp of the major principles of the discipline, and I need to know how to ask the right questions—how to hold up a puzzling bit of reality or its residue, be certain the puzzle is understood, and wait . . . wait while the learner pokes and prods, turns the puzzle this way and that, shakes it, holds it up to the light, speculates, rejects, decides it has no solution, then suddenly sees something not seen before—a relationship, a pattern, an implication. It's sometimes harder to let students do that if you're an expert on the subject.

Thinking

Most students have acquired some relatively rigid ideas about what is supposed to happen in school. Since what I do in class may not always meet their expectations, I've found it useful to warn them by sharing with them my reasons for departing from some of the traditional practices.

I'll often use a simple exercise to create a basis for discussion of one of the peculiarities of my approach to teaching. Without prior discussion, I'll ask them to write, on an unsigned scrap of paper, a couple of typical exam or quiz questions—any subject, any grade level. If they can't remember a question they've been asked, I'll tell them to "make them up, but try to make them just the sort of questions you've grown accustomed to being asked by school teachers." I collect the responses, put them aside, and begin a discussion of what teachers really mean when they make statements such as "In *my* class, you're really going to have to *think!*"

In the interests of precision in our discussion, I then help students break the word *think* down into a Benjamin Bloom – like taxonomy of specific thinking processes—inferring, hypothesizing, generalizing, recalling, categorizing, synthesizing, and so on. With the taxonomy on the blackboard, I then begin reading aloud their examples of typical examination questions, asking them to identify the particular thinking process students would probably use to answer each. When they decide, I place a tally mark after the appropriate word on the list.

Inferring   /
Categorizing   //
Hypothesizing
Generalizing
Recalling   ‖‖ ‖‖‖‖ ‖‖ ‖‖ ‖‖ //
Synthesizing   ///
Valuing   /

I have not yet been surprised by the result. What has always emerged is a picture of the cognitive narrowness of much traditional instruction. After the word *recalling*, there is invariably a far larger cluster of marks than after any

other word. I can then point out the fact that if I am successful in my effort
to get them to "think"—to engage in a *full* range of cognitive processes—
they are going to be doing something they have not always done in previous
classes.

We then talk about the emotional reactions they may have to classwork
that requires using a variety of mental processes, and about specific reasons
for those reactions. For example, at least some students will eventually react
to the work with a vague feeling that "this isn't education." Perfectly understandable. After years of equating education primarily with the simple process of storing and recalling information, anything else will not be defined as
education. Sometimes, understandably, the students who object the most to
being required to engage in a wide range of thinking processes are those who
have been the most successful in playing the relatively simple game of "How
much do you remember?" Specific reactions can be anticipated. Some students,
after a few days, will say, "Please! Just tell me what you want me to know!"
or, "We're not getting anywhere!" or, "This is so disorganized!" or, "Could
we have a worksheet to fill out?" Other students will react differently. Because
they are not involved in an attempt to remember several dozen or hundred
bits of information, they will consider the work easy or soft. Others will feel
that, for the first time, they have hold of something really challenging.

Incidentally, the problems associated with deliberate expansion and diver-
sification of thought processes shouldn't be underestimated. Students aren't
the only ones who may react negatively. Many parents, teachers, and
administrators also think of education as primarily a matter of information
storage and recall—a sort of monster game of Trivial Pursuit (and believe that,
if students aren't being required to think in class, the whole problem can be
eliminated with an assigned term paper, thesis, or dissertation).

These people aren't going to be understanding or supportive. But their
fears and apprehensions are different from those of the students. They will tend
to tell you that what you're attempting to help students do is admirable, but
your first obligation is to conform to established practice, so as to perpetuate
the system. They won't use those words, of course. They will simply remind
you of the immediacy of the next mandated standardized examination, and
of your obligation to make certain that your students pass it with the highest
possible scores. And your students *will* have to do that. The critics are not likely
to be receptive to suggestions that much traditional instruction is most
accurately characterized as ritual.

The happiest solution is of course to integrate, to devise ways to use the
traditional content as a vehicle for involving students in activities which require
them to engage in a full range of cognitive processes. Unfortunately, that isn't

generally an easy task. As I'll note presently in comments about textbooks, much traditional instructional material is organized in ways which make it almost impossible for students to do much else but read and try to remember what they've read.

I try to integrate, but if I can't I simply identify the standard course content and devise some way to deal with it efficiently. After we've discussed the necessity of meeting societal expectations, I may direct the students to a good commercial outline, assign that which needs to be memorized as homework, or present them with a summary and some mnemonic devices for dealing with information likely to appear on the standardized test. With a little planning, the demands of tradition can usually be met in five or ten minutes of efficiently organized class time.

Metaphors

Occasionally, to help prepare students for the instruction ahead, we'll talk about their conceptions of the teaching and learning process. It's very likely that they share the usual metaphors about the processes of learning—that their heads are "empty containers," and knowledge is "stuff" to be somehow gotten inside those containers. We employ such figures of speech constantly, of course, because we know so little about how the mind really works. Eventually we stop thinking about our education-related metaphors as feeble attempts to describe something extremely complex and come to see them as the process itself. When that happens, activity that doesn't mesh with our metaphors probably won't be seen as educational.

If our metaphors for educating were reasonably parallel to that which we are trying to describe, there would be few problems. Unfortunately, they aren't. They suggest that the processes of learning are simple; they imply, for example, that teaching and learning involve merely a transfer of something quantitative. Knowledge is an entity that can be "divided" into "bits" to be "passed on," "taken in," "absorbed," "stored." Teachers "cover the material." We "cram" to prepare for an examination. Familiar metaphors for educating tend to be some version of spoon-feeding—an adult selecting food, preparing it, bringing it to the child, cutting it into pieces, determining the sequence of presentation, picking up the individual pieces, and putting them in the child's mouth. All the child has to do is swallow and keep it down.

I raise questions about these usual ways of thinking about educating: "Suppose the process is more like, say, making love? Should that be the case, wouldn't actions and attitudes now considered perfectly appropriate and effective be unacceptable (might even have negative consequences)?" The spoon feeding metaphor suggests that in teaching and learning one participant is very active, the other passive. But if educating is more like lovemaking, questions are raised about those roles. The two metaphors put in a different light questions that are central to educating, questions about authority, respect, passion, expertise, involvement, even attendance.

Neither of the metaphors is adequate (although the second is probably more helpful than the first), so we discuss others. It may be that education, the objective of which is the expansion of understanding, is more a matter of closing a circuit, building a bridge, going inside to examine the skeleton, climbing an observation tower, forging a link, tracing a blueprint, or stacking blocks in different ways. We'll talk about a metaphor I use more frequently— that of rearranging mental furniture. The word *rearranging* is helpful to me. I don't know how valid the idea is, but I seem to accomplish more if I assume that everything students need to know in order to understand is already in their heads. My task is to wander around with them in their mental attics and basements, find what is needed at the moment, bring it out, dust it off, see how it's put together, then suggest where it could go to be in the most useful and meaningful relationship with everything else.

Conceptual Scaffolds

In the chapter 1 comments about the inadequacies of the traditional general education curriculum, I touched briefly on its lack of conceptual organization. We know that the mind can't handle very much random information. To be stored, recalled, and *used,* information must be placed within a conceptual structure. Related ideas must be labeled and stored together in a category, related categories labeled and stored together in more general categories, these more general categories in turn labeled and stored together, and so on. The ultimate objective, of course, is a totally integrated knowledge structure, a structure in which everything known is tied together in a mutually supportive, logical framework.

Constructing conceptual frameworks which integrate knowledge is what educating for understanding is all about. Surprisingly, educators and educational critics have very little to say about such structures. It seems to be assumed that if students are simply exposed to information, in some automatic or magical way the information will organize and integrate itself. Unfortunately, it won't. Instruction may dump a load of bricks in the student's intellectual yard, and the student may stack some of them for a purpose of need or interest, but if a structure of complexity and consequence is built the present curriculum deserves little credit.

Helping students construct formal, integrated conceptual structures that represent reality is no small challenge. Unfortunately, at present it's a challenge most teachers must meet on their own. In few fields are the professionals who shape the academic versions of disciplines interested in either the overall discipline structure or in the integration of their discipline with other disciplines. Teachers who understand cognitive structure, who know that big, powerful, abstract ideas are built on successive layers of ideas of lesser generality and greater concreteness will, in most disciplines, have to devise for themselves approaches to the task of helping students build those structures.

Incidentally, if the complexity and sophistication of this task were generally understood, it would lay to rest forever the notion that good teaching requires mostly a knowledge of the subject. It might also alter the popular view that schools of education have no important role to play in the training of teachers. They certainly do. If education courses fail, it's not primarily because teaching is such a simple process that methods courses are unnecessary. A far more likely explanation is that they fail because of the inherent complexity of the processes of educating, and many of the teachers and students who face each other in education courses simply aren't up to the task. Complicating the work is the fact that students come to methods courses after years of observing teaching based on simplistic notions of what it's all about. It isn't reasonable to expect that two or three methods courses (even very good ones) can erase perceptions of teaching reinforced by twenty or thirty thousand hours of experience, then replace them with unfamiliar skills more complex than those required in medicine or law.

The whole process is further complicated by much of the instruction students continue to witness when they reach the university. More than at any other level, it is there that teaching is perceived as simply a matter of sitting students down and talking at them. Research, not teaching, is what the university is primarily about. Someone has pointed out that university faculty talk of "research opportunities" and "teaching loads." The perspective is usually apparent.

Textbooks

To many students, nothing seems more central to education than the textbook. Teachers, administrators, classrooms, laboratories, gymnasiums, blackboards, desks, projectors, computers, notebooks—each has a place and plays a role, but the textbook is considered the sine qua non of the educating process.

Textbooks are *the* symbol of education. Some measure of their perceived importance is indicated by the action and attitudes of our society related to them. Parents demand that they be brought home from school. Many teachers won't start classes without them. Academic departments will adopt new textbooks and then spend weeks reorganizing courses, as if the change in books had somehow altered the field of study. Administrators sometimes think that all books for a class should be the same, and that all classes using a book should be on approximately the same page on the same day. Elaborate and expensive procedures are devised to select them. Angry crowds sometimes burn them, and not infrequently the courts are asked to make judgements about them. Obviously, textbooks are thought to be very important.

To suggest that traditional textbooks are a major, perhaps *the* major obstacle to the achievement of educational excellence will seem to many to be nothing less than heresy. It's acceptable to find fault with textbooks, to criticize the uninspired writing, the "dumbing down" of vocabulary, the concern for comprehensiveness at the expense of depth and clarity, spiraling cost, the usual several years' lag behind current knowledge, the dreary sameness stemming from publishers' attempts to duplicate the current best-seller. But to suggest that in most disciplines the textbooks actually stand in the way of major educational improvement is to risk being labeled as too eccentric to be taken seriously.

Students have adopted society's general attitudes toward textbooks and textbooklike materials. For this reason, since I make very little use of textbooks (use them at all only under administrative duress), I have to go to considerable lengths to explain why. One of the problems, I tell them, is the conventional textbook's expository style—the thousands of words "telling you what's true." Typically, textbooks read like this:

posed the farmers on many political issues, but these two groups were united in their opposition to the spread of slavery. Not only was slavery abolished as a result of the Civil War, but legislation passed during the war fulfilled eastern demands for a high tariff and stronger banks, as well as western demands for free land and federal aid to railroads. Thus the Republicans enjoyed the support of several groups owing it gratitude: freedmen, manufacturers, officers banks, fa

effects occur the vicinity of a wire carrying an alternating current signal. One of these effects is that both an electric field and a magnetic field are created around the conductor. The magnetic field can induce the signal it is carrying into adjacent conductors. In communications, the induced and unwanted signal is called "crosstalk." However, if one conductor of the pair ground side of the circuit, and is made other conductor, both the radio the magnetic field can b

What most textbooks offer the student is a kind of residue of a discipline. The words in the text have been preceded by decades or centuries of thought, argument, exploration, criticism, organizing, and reorganizing. Out of all this has come conclusions, often several thousand of them. Summaries of those conclusions provide most of the content of the usual textbook.

Now for reference purposes, such a resource is useful. There needs to be a handy place to store the distilled thinking of scholars within a discipline, and until the time arrives when the student can conveniently access reference material from a computer terminal or a similar source, a book is probably the most appropriate device.

The difficulties arise from the assumption that what's basically a reference work is a proper tool for instruction. It isn't. Outside the field of education, it's assumed that a serious book written to educate will dwell for its entire length on the development, illustration, and application of a single idea. Textbooks, however, present not one idea but a veritable tidal wave of them. Some of those ideas may be powerful, but they are mixed indiscriminately with vast numbers which aren't. This mass of information, presented as it usually is without anything approaching an adequate conceptual structure, is simply overwhelming to the average student. The mind is flooded with ideas which are inert because there isn't time to develop them. As a consequence, most are soon forgotten.

The second problem is more fundamental. Because the content of the conventional expository text is primarily a compendium of conclusions, all the significant thinking has already been done. It's very much like giving the student a vast crossword puzzle with all the blanks filled in. There's nothing left to do except perhaps memorize it—a task not likely to generate enthusiasm or sharpen the intellect.

What the student being introduced to a discipline needs is not an encyclopedic overview of conclusions (even if they were able to cope with such a volume of information). They need to know with what part of reality that discipline is concerned, need to have a firm grasp of the major ideas and idea relationships which organize thinking about that part of reality, and need to know how to engage in the processes by means of which those ideas and idea relationships are generated, evaluated, refined, expanded, integrated.

Here's an example of traditional textbook content, and content in a form that requires the learner to use a wide range of thought processes of the kind that underlie the expansion of knowledge. The examples are from the discipline of history, but the differences they illustrate are applicable to every field of knowledge.

LEARNING ABOUT
A SOURCE OF
AMERICAN VALUES
USING EXPOSITION

What were the Puritans like? Many of
their ways of acting grew out of their
religious beliefs. They felt that all people were basically evil, and that only a
strict observance of God's laws as presented in the Bible could keep this evil
tendency under control. . .

LEARNING ABOUT A
SOURCE OF AMERICAN
VALUES USING
"RESIDUE"

Below is the alphabet as it was taught to Puritan children in the New England Primer. What seem to be
important Puritan beliefs?

A — In *Adam's* Fall
We Sinned all.

B — Thy Life to Mend
This *Book* Attend.

C — The *Cat* doth play
And after slay.

D — A *Dog* will bite
A *Thief* at night.

E — An *Eagles* flight
Is out of sight.

F — The Idle *Fool*
Is whipt at School.

Textbooks which encourage students to use a full range of cognitive processes occasionally appear. I know from first-hand experience as a writer of them that they enjoy little success. Ironically, although such textbooks allow students to learn in a manner far more natural than that permitted by conventional exposition, textbooks containing mostly primary data are considered too unorthodox to be acceptable. Until this attitude changes, until there is general understanding of the ways in which traditional textbooks get in the way of intellectual growth by short-circuiting most cognitive processes except recall, textbooks will continue to block improvement in instruction.

Textbooks can be vastly improved, but even those which move beyond the narrow bounds of traditional exposition are less-than-ideal tools for teaching. Education is, after all, about the real world. Textbooks are supposed to help explain parts of the real world—rocks, schizophrenia, inflation, language, vertebrates. In order to "two-dimensionalize" an aspect of reality so it will fit into the pages of a book, the author must select, freeze, flatten, sterilize, organize, abstract. By the time the original is in a form appropriate for the pages of a textbook, it's a pale and shallow shadow four or five steps removed from that which it represents. In my opinion, textbooks should be used as a primary instructional tool only when it's impossible to touch the real thing or its tangible residue. On the wall of every classroom, in letters too large for the teacher to ignore, I'd like to see Alfred North Whitehead's words quoted earlier: "The second-handedness of the learned world is the secret of its mediocrity."

One more observation: From traditional assumptions about the efficacy of the textbook comes what must surely be the most mind-numbing of all classroom activities—"filling in the blank." Sentences from textbooks are reproduced in workbooks or on worksheets, but with words missing. Millions of student hours annually are spent in the dreary search of textbooks for parallel sentences providing the missing words. In many schools, particularly in some of the newer, sectarian ones, students may sit for hours each day in individual study carrels transferring words from textbook to workbook. It is an utter waste of time and children.

Evaluation

As soon as I suggest to students that what happens in class may differ somewhat from what they've come to expect, for many of them the most important concern about school quickly surfaces. They want to know about grades and examinations.

As I've said, years of reinforcement lie behind most students' assumption that "learning" means "remembering." It follows then that at examination time they expect some form of the question, How much do you recall? Students may not enjoy the task of remembering, and they may agree in a discussion that instruction that has that as its goal is narrow and superficial, but that doesn't mean that they don't prefer examinations of memory over almost everything else. They do.

I used to try to explore examination and grading theories and philosophies with students, but I've about given it up. I haven't had much success in explaining to them (or to teachers, administrators, state legislators, or anyone else) my fears about where our infatuation with measurement is taking us. There seems to be little appreciation of the extreme danger to genuine education in the present drive toward "accountability." Preoccupied with the race toward the goals which the test makers can measure, we're ignoring the far more important goals which they cannot. There are no tests which can establish the degree of achievement of the goals of general education. The number of correct words per minute a student can type can be counted, but there is no way to precisely determine that student's progress in understanding self. Whether or not a student can write a technically correct sentence can be established, but there are no objective measures of the satisfaction that can stem from having fashioned a beautiful phrase. A test can easily be devised to establish that a student knows the names of the planets and their relative distance from the sun. But whether or not instruction has made the student more curious about the nature of the universe and the place of humans in it is an assessment that lies beyond the test maker's skill.

So I keep the comments about evaluation to a minimum, perhaps suggesting merely that my goals for testing aren't much different from those they accept in a mathematics course. On a math exam, one doesn't expect to be asked to do the same problems used in class for explanatory purposes. One is supposed to have learned a process, and the ability to engage in that process is what is tested.

Objectives

There is, of course, the matter of objectives. I may or may not bring the subject up. If I do, I'll probably simply ask, "Why are you here?" and from the responses ("My parents make me come," "I want to graduate," "I want to be successful") we begin to talk about objectives—student objectives, not course objectives. (Courses don't have objectives.) If students' overriding concerns at the moment are to be liked, to make lots of money, to get ahead at work or be happy, we make these objectives as explicit as possible. The task is then to demonstrate relationships between their objectives and the course in history, the humanities, the sciences, or other study that lies ahead.

This really isn't so difficult, for every objective students can think of must be achieved in the context of one or another sociocultural system or subsystem. They can either, through the discipline at hand, increase their understanding of the systems of which they are a part and enjoy the benefits of that understanding, or they can fail to increase their understanding and be less well prepared to get what they want out of life. (Unfortunately, the fact that the course content can help students realize their objectives doesn't necessarily mean that they will be motivated. Not every student who has a goal is willing to work for it. There will probably always be students who just can't be reached.)

Putting It Together

Of course, none of what I've been saying is new. The five or six pedagogical elements I see as central to my approach to teaching—concern for the physical environment, emphasis on the here and now and the tangible rather than on second- and third-hand information, the requirement that students use a wide range of thought processes, seeing myself in the role of colearner, the adoption of more accurate metaphors to represent the teaching and learning process, the creation of a conceptual framework as the central intellectual task, acceptance of the legitimacy of real student goals and an attempt to work with them—these are all very old ideas. From time to time one or the other of them appears under a new name, its validity is established, it is discussed for three or four years, and some segment of the educational establishment will try to implement it.

The effort fails. I think it fails because it isn't recognized that *all the elements are interdependent*, that *all must be in place before any one of them can succeed*. The inquiry movement in the 1960s and 1970s illustrates the point. Of *course* learning through inquiry is valid and natural. Humans have been learning that way since they've been human. But this most-natural approach to learning couldn't make it into the classroom using conventional textbooks, with the traditional concern for "covering the material," with tests which ask only, "How much can you remember?" in a physical environment that told students to sit passively and listen to teachers who believed that teaching was mostly a matter of telling students what they were supposed to know. Everything has to work in support of everything else.

My general pessimism about the future of education in America stems primarily from my belief that it is almost impossible to get the educational establishment to accept, simultaneously, so many ideas so at odds with present practice.

The Main Task

What I'm trying to do, of course, is to raise the students' awareness of the concept of culture, then help them build mental models for that concept which are equal to the task of making sense of daily experience.

I don't have answers to most of the questions about the best sequence for instruction. Should one start small, observing, say, individual actions within one's own experience until the concept of 'patterns of action' emerges? Does one then follow the same procedure with cultural premises, environment, and demographics, assembling and combining subconcepts until the general concept of sociocultural system finally takes shape?

I'm not certain. I've done that—started small, with the specifics, and worked toward the general. I've done the reverse. I've started in the middle and worked both ways. Right now I seem to have the most success attacking the problem whole. However, because of the level of abstractness of that which is being studied, and the lack of student background in it, I often begin actual instruction with a parallel but simpler task. I may divide the class into work teams and tell them, "Construct an outline or conceptual tree that we can use to study, compare, describe, analyze . . . bicycles."

Something like this usually emerges:

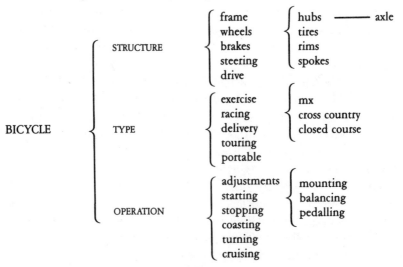

"OK," I say, "what you've done for bicycles we're going to try to do for something larger and with more moving parts—things called 'sociocultural systems.' Sociocultural systems are collections of people who occupy the same general area, act in similar ways, and share important states of mind. You're generally familiar with them, but your thoughts about them probably aren't organized. We're going to try to organize them (rearrange your mental furniture) in much the same way that you organized what you know about bicycles. Some examples of sociocultural systems are the Amish, Apaches, Armenians, Athenians, Aztecs, etc." (During this stage of instruction, I try to avoid mention of large political entities which usually contain many different, overlapping systems and subsystems. We'll get to these later, when our analytical concepts are more firmly grounded.) I then say, "Get with your team members and see if you can do for sociocultural systems what you did for bicycles—put together an outline we can use to study any society, anytime, anywhere."

Construction of a model now begins. I participate as little as possible, mostly asking very general questions designed to help team members think about the task in broad terms. We'll probably talk about the fish-would-be-the-last-to-discover-water problem, and of the applicability of that problem to their task. We may also discuss how previous schooling has structured their thinking, causing them to be more aware of certain kinds of information (for example, political and economic) than of other kinds.

We make much use of the blackboard. Teams put their ideas about model components alongside those of other teams and argue their relative merit until there is general understanding and agreement on the categories and subcategories of a model.

Through all of this I have the current version of my own model in mind, of course, but I try to avoid comments which might unduly structure discussion. Since my model is so much a product of work by earlier classes, I assume that if students are allowed sufficient latitude the model will continue to evolve.

Once we have a tentative model, we can begin to exploit its potential. To the extent that time permits, I build activities around each of the subcomponents within demographics, environment, patterns of action, and cultural premises, making maximum use of concrete, daily, here-and-now experience and contrasts drawn from other societies. If time is very limited we'll concentrate on those parts of the model most closely related to the traditional course content, touching on the rest of the components only briefly.

I try never to get very far away from reminders of the fact that it is ourselves and the world around us we're trying to understand. We're not engaged in just another academic exercise, but are using the most direct means at our disposal for getting in touch with fundamental sources of happiness and unhappiness, security and insecurity, peace and conflict, and other basic human concerns.

Appendix B. Illustrative Instructional Material

Since I believe the entire general education curriculum needs to be reworked, I wish I could lay out a complete K – 14 scope and sequence. Unfortunately, I don't know enough to do that, and even if I did have the necessary expertise, the exercise would almost certainly be a waste of time. As I've said, I'm convinced that institutionalization in American education is now so far advanced that change of real consequence is out of the question. Even my suggestion that the concept of culture merits consideration as a basis for integrating the curriculum has drawn from some reviewers startlingly rancorous responses and a refusal to seriously consider the proposal.

I don't think the system is going to change. My primary interest, therefore, is in providing individual science, mathematics, humanities, social science, language, and other teachers with a conceptual structure that will allow them to put their disciplines in perspective. I've tried to show the practical benefits which can be realized—the identification of presently neglected areas of study, criteria for sorting out the significant from the less significant, solid conceptual bridges to other disciplines and other parts of reality, a cognitive framework that logically integrates everything, a tool for endlessly expanding knowledge through the exploration of relationships, and evidence of the superficiality of much present evaluation.

My hope is to reach at least some classroom teachers. Perhaps it will help if I can show how the model translates into practical classroom activity that meets all the criteria I've established, fits within the bounds of present courses, and can be organized by individual teachers without outside help or support.

On the following pages are a few examples of activities I've used in working with junior high, high school, and university students. I've tried to choose examples which, with minor alterations in emphasis, would be appropriate in several different disciplines.

I'll begin with patterns of action activities, then proceed through cultural premises, demographics, environment, and systemic relationships and change.

Patterns of Action

In the study of patterns of action, detail is everything. It may seem that requiring students to see and describe almost every physical movement in a pattern is to be concerned with the obvious and the trivial, but that is far from the case. The student writing about patterns for worship who says "the ushers" is simply not seeing as much as the student who writes, "four adult males." In this small difference are implications worth noting. "Children go to bed about 8:00" says far less than "The mother puts the children to bed about 8:00."

I may push the same papers back four or five times in an effort to help students see more than is first apparent. I think there's real merit both in their being asked to *really* see that of which human experience is made, and in trying to describe it with the utmost precision.

Patterns for Pairing

Assignment: Describe a procedure used by you and your friends for meeting those of the opposite sex.

Jennifer Napier from Eau Gallie High School responds:

> Hanging out in the mall is one good way to find a guy. A group of girls (usually from two to four of us) will get together on a Friday or Saturday night and head for the mall.

> When we get there, we don't usually go in the stores. We choose a place to start and then walk all the way around the mall, just going in the shops where guys are most likely to be. Record stores are very popular for meeting people. A girl may spot a guy thumbing through records of her favorite artists and she'll go over to where he is standing and start a conversation about them.

> If the record store isn't a success, then it's off to the video game room. Guys and girls wander around watching people play. Sometimes the token machine is a good place to strike up a conversation.

> The final place to check out is the courtyard—the big area where there are lots of little restaurants with seats and tables placed in the middle. We'll walk around pretending we're trying to decide where to eat, but really checking out the crowd. If it looks like there are some possibilities, we get something to eat and find a table as near as possible to the guys.

As an isolated exercise, a description of a teenage, middle-class pattern for meeting members of the opposite sex may seem too narrow and trivial to be of value. However, the activity has many uses. The student is demonstrating a grasp of the general concept of social pattern, and of one component of a conceptual network that, it should now be clear, is vast and versatile. It is an easy step to similar descriptions of other patterns of action within her native society. Each of these patterns is related to the other patterns, to the dominant value structure of the society, to the system environment, and to demographic characteristics. As understanding of each of these components grows, the capacity for relationship exploration expands and her understanding of the society of which she is a part expands with it. In addition, of course, once this basic conceptual structure is in place, it is available for use to expand understanding of any sociocultural system, anywhere, anytime, with the student's understanding of her own society serving as a source of clarifying contrast. In fact, I usually pair the above activity with a handout containing a conversation between several Indian teenagers describing the excitement and security of a pattern for pairing in which parents play the major role.

In most classes, we'll identify fifteen or twenty major patterns of action. Since each of these patterns is composed of many subpatterns, it isn't possible to study them all. The usual procedure is to choose those patterns most central to the course under study, then break them down and down until a level is reached that is sufficiently circumscribed in time and space to permit a relatively brief pattern description. ("Patterns for pairing" is one of the many patterns which collectively are labeled "patterns for maintaining membership" on the model.) The general "patterns for work" could be broken down to "industrial work," then to "factory production work," and finally to "assembly line work." At this level, precise answers to the action-and-interaction pattern-identifying questions—who is doing what, with whom, where, when, how, with what?— become possible. When another component of the model is broken down to the same level of generality, it is then possible to begin speculating about possible relationships. For example, how might assembly line work relate to cultural premises regarding the nature of the self? To patterns for socializing? To population distribution? To constructions?

Patterns for Communicating

I've pinned to the bulletin board three clusters of large ads from the real estate section of Sunday's paper. All the ads are for new, single-family dwellings. One cluster of ads is for houses in relatively low-cost subdivisions, one for middle-income housing, and the third for areas where very expensive houses are being built.

Assignment: Study the ads for the next three or four hours. They communicate different kinds of messages to different kinds of people in different kinds of ways. Even from where you're sitting, and with the prices blanked out, you can probably tell the difference. Note, for example, the contrast in the amount of unused white space. Ask and answer as many questions about the clusters as you can—questions about words, about sentences, about style, about everything. Identify every language-related respect in which the clusters differ from each other, and develop explanations of those differences.

Cultural Premises

Designing instructional activities for cultural premises is more difficult than for other components of the model. Demographic characteristics can be represented graphically and statistically. The environment can be touched, measured, photographed, mapped. Patterns of action can be observed directly. But states of mind must always be inferred. Designing participative activities which make students aware of their time orientation, their assumptions about causation, their premises about the nature of the self, and the other beliefs and values that underlie their behavior can be a real challenge.

The activities I use to help students better understand cultural premises are generally of two kinds. I'll try to clarify a belief or value either by contrasting it with a variation on the premise held by another society, or by having students infer the existence of a premise by observing patterns and regularities within their own society.

Here's an example of an activity that uses cultural contrast to help students get a clearer picture of one of their premises related to the self. (The description was given to me by Dr. William Bernatzsky, a Jesuit Brother teaching in rural Korea.)

Traditional Korean Funerals

A low table with a bowl of uncooked rice on it is placed before the main gate of the house in which a death has occurred. It is to keep out the evil spirits which want to take the place of the soul in the body of the dead.

The body is placed in the coffin, which is placed on blocks in the main heated-floor room (*an pang*) of the house.

The sons and other relatives (up to second cousins) of the deceased greet the mourners and are expected to wail with an unrestrained show of grief, repeating five times a customary Korean exclamation for pain, "A-i-gu, a-i-gu, a-i-gu, a-i-gu. a-i-gu." Others in the room respond with "O-i, o-i, o-i."

Visitors first enter the room and bow deeply to the spirit of the soul that still remains with the corpse. Men make two deep *kow-tows*, each preceded by the circular movement of the joined hands known as the *up*.

The chief mourner may wear a wide wicker hat, like a shallow basket about two feet in diameter. This hat, worn mainly in summer, keeps most of the upper part of his face in shadow. It symbolizes the shame the son feels at allowing his parent to die, which makes him hide his face from heaven. He also carries a staff of paulownia wood if he is mourning for his mother, or of bamboo if for his father.

After bowing to the soul at the coffin, the mourners go outside and bow once to the sons and other close relatives. They may say some words of sympathy. Then they go to help with the meal or funeral preparations or to visit with other mourners.

If a child dies, no funeral is held. The father simply puts the body in a straw bag and, possibly accompanied by one or two male relatives or other men, buries it in some isolated place. There is no ceremony.

(a) In this description, what Korean pattern of action is most unlike your own? (b) What premise seems to underlie the Korean pattern? (c) With what premise of yours is the Korean premise in conflict? (d) What are some American policies, programs, or policies which probably stem from your culture's premise on this matter?

A student responds:

The differing pattern is that they don't have funeral services for children. Maybe the death rate is high and so death is common and they don't think much about it when a child dies. Someone in my work group thinks Koreans believe humanness is something you learn as you get older instead of something you're born with.

Whatever the reason, they don't seem to think children are as important or worth as much as adults, and that's a premise unlike mine and most people in my society.

Evidences of our premise:

—We have funerals for children, and people are sometimes even sadder than they are at funerals for adults.

—People will pay large amounts of money to adopt infants. Sometimes you read about babies being stolen.

—We have lots of laws about equal rights, equal opportunity, equal protection, etc. I'm sure these apply to children in the same way they apply to adults.

Our cultural premises become clearer when placed alongside contrasting ones from other societies. Premises can also be inferred from an analysis of regularities within a society. For example, sometimes I'll have my students write a relatively lengthy description of what they think (or hope) life will be like for them twenty or twenty-five years in the future. I'll put the papers aside, then engage in a series of activities designed to help them clarify their own

society's view of the good life. What emerges in most American classrooms is
a list that looks something like this:

It's good to:

—Move up
—Be your own boss
—Own lots of stuff
—Be young, thin, active, and attractive
—Win
—Not be too different
—Satisfy wants quickly
—Be mobile

When the list is complete, I'll return the papers completed earlier and
have students underline comments which relate to middle-class American
cultural assumptions about the good life.

Here's the opening paragraphs of one such paper, with underlining:

It's the first week in April, 2010, and my husband and I have stored the cars
and the helicopter and are ready for our usual Spring move from our hilltop
home on the island of Kauai to our apartment in Manhattan. We're going back
a week early this year for final fittings for new outfits I'm having made. Since
my dressmaker has my measurements (which haven't changed since I was 18),
the fittings shouldn't take very long.

I need the outfits to wear to the International Interior Design Awards weekend
in Brussels. The design firm I own has won First Place for my designs for the
interiors of a new Performing Arts Center in Atlanta.

My husband and I will be attending the affair week after next. After that we'll
join our son and daughter for three or four days of skiing in Switzerland.

When students analyze what they've written, most discover that they've
been rather thoroughly programmed by their society.

With activities like this, I try to help students clarify their assumptions
about causation, nature, space, trends—all the major premises which underlie
their behavior.

Here's a more difficult assignment:

Societies are, at their most fundamental level, the sum of the states of mind
their members share. These shared ideas, beliefs, assumptions, premises, and
values underlie and explain, insofar as explanation is possible, the actions and
feelings of members.

One set of ideas within every society's cognitive system has to do with time. Since time is such an abstract idea, there are great variations in how different societies perceive it. And of course from these differing perceptions of the nature of time, differing approaches to life follow.

Using dialogue from modern American fiction, television soap opera, and daily experience as major sources of data, collect words, phrases, figures of speech, idiomatic expressions, grammatical constructions—any aspect of the language that relates to and therefore possibly discloses your society's concept of the nature of time (shape, size, essence, value—everything).

Devise category systems for organizing the data, then explore how the conceptions manifest themselves in daily experience and behavior in your society.

Environment

In the pursuit of an understanding of the general concept of environment and its more specific component *constructions,* I might begin by having students organize the classroom furniture in different ways, then speculate about the effects of the various physical arrangements on action, attitudes, and feelings.

Sometimes I clear a space in a corner of the classroom, provide a desk and two chairs, and have several different students arrange the three pieces of furniture as they would in a private office of their own. As each student moves the furniture to some different, preferred position, another student draws each arrangement on the blackboard. The results usually look something like this:

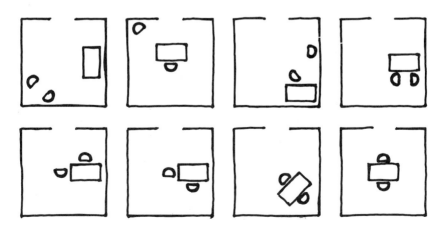

We then discuss the implications of the various arrangements—what each suggests about the arranger, and how particular ways of organizing an office can structure interaction and foster certain ideas and attitudes.

Here's a more elaborate activity designed to help students think about relationships between constructions and human behavior:

> Divide a sheet of paper with a vertical line. Title the left side of the sheet "1900–1925," and the right side "1950–1975."

> Examine typical middle-class suburban housing of each era (for example, the area from the river back to about 10th Street for the earlier era; Royal Oak subdivision for the second). Identify differences in design and siting of structures and other human-made features of each area. If you can, describe the 1900–1925 neighborhood as it was during that period of time. List the contrasting physical characteristics of the two areas, then discuss those you believe have implications for (a) intrafamily relationships, and (b) interfamily relationships.

Here's an example of a response to the assignment:

1900-1925	1950-1975
Mostly two-story houses	Mostly one-story houses
Large front porches	No front porches
Large glass area in front door	No glass, or peepholes in door
Sidewalks	No sidewalks
Large, openable windows with screens	Fixed windows, or small windows not usually opened
One bath upstairs or outside toilet	Two bathrooms
Small bedrooms with bed and chest	Larger bedrooms, multipurpose, with bed, chest, desk, TV
Bedrooms in same part of house	Split bedroom plan
50-foot lots	80-foot lots
Attics	Crawl space only
Detached garages	Attached garages, many with door openers
(Originally) stove in kitchen and living room	Central heat and air-conditioning
Alleys	No alleys
Trash-burning barrels in back	Trash pickup
Outside clothesline	Dryer in garage
Average 20-foot setback of house from street	Average 45-foot setback of house from street
Low-profile landscaping	High-profile landscaping on all sides of houses

Intrafamily Relationships

Since there was just one bathroom in the 1900s houses, there would have been more family contact in that area. The bedrooms were all in the same area, which could have had the same effect. (Little children wouldn't have felt isolated as they probably do now in split-plan houses.) In the houses without central heat, most family members were probably together in the kitchen or living room when it was cold. Even when it wasn't cold, the bedrooms weren't as liveable as they are in a lot of newer houses (with their own chairs, desks, TVs, phones, bathrooms, etc.) so the family was more likely to be together downstairs. Studying and sewing were probably done in the dining room instead of in bedrooms.

Interfamily Relationships

Almost everything about the neighborhood we studied has something to do with interfamily relationships. The 1900s house sort of opened people to other people. The houses were close to the street, and a sidewalk led straight up to the front porch. There was furniture on the porch. People sat there in full view of other people. Even when they went inside there was so much glass around the front door they could still be seen. If it was summer, the windows were all open and you could probably hear the neighbors, tell what was going on and probably smell what they were having to eat. The houses were close to the street and close together too, and had big windows just a few feet away from the windows of the houses on each side. Usually there wasn't any trees or shrubbery in between. Most of the houses had (and still have) detached garages located on an alley behind the house. To get to the garage you had to go ouside. Drying clothes and taking out the trash also required going outside, with more chances of running into the neighbors. Because the houses sit on the front of the lots there is room out back. There aren't many gardens there now, but probably there used to be a lot of them. That would also put them in close contact with their neighbors.

As with all activities, it's important to keep attention directed toward the big picture. Understanding relationships between human behavior and the configuration of classrooms, offices, and neighborhoods is not the primary objective. These are but means to the end of understanding a general proposition. The shape of cities, the direction of highways, the size of cathedrals, the nature of monuments—these are all constructions, and are potential sources of an understanding of ourselves and others.

Demographics

The concepts within demographics are relatively simple and easily understood. If I design instructional activities around them, it's generally not so much to explain the components as to show that seemingly mundane characteristics of sociocultural systems, such as the age distribution of members or the ratio of males to females, is in fact important to an understanding of how a society is functioning.

Here's an example of an activity built around the population distribution component of demographics:

> Most of you have lived in this area for at least several years. Some of you, I know, were born here. All of you have some familiarity with what's called "downtown"—that part of Main Street between the South Hill Viaduct and Five Points, and including two or three blocks to the east and west.
>
> As I talk about it, you probably have some mental images of the area—images of wide, almost empty sidewalks, relatively light traffic and plenty of empty parking spaces, some pawn shops, used-furniture stores and other similar businesses, and empty windows covered up with plywood or paper.
>
> It wasn't always like that. Some of your parents remember when it wasn't like that at all. Here's a picture from an old newspaper taken in 1949 of about three blocks of Main Street on a Tuesday morning in October—just an ordinary day. The population of the city was a lot lower then, and there were a lot fewer cars, but look at the traffic and the crowds on the sidewalk!
>
> What happened? One of the components of our model—population distribution—explains a lot. What happened was something called "suburbanization," and it had all kinds of unexpected effects for which no one at the time was prepared.
>
> Tear a sheet of paper into pieces about two inches square. You'll need eight pieces altogether. On each slip, copy one of the following phrases:
>
> Decrease in fire, police protection
> Construction of suburban malls
> Declining city tax receipts
> Population movement to the suburbs
> Decreased demand for downtown locations
> Increase in crime
> Decrease in downtown business
> Decrease in downtown property values
>
> Now put the slips in a circle, starting with "Population movement to the suburbs" in the 12 o'clock position. Choose the slip which best describes the probable first consequence of this population movement and put it in the 1:30 position. Continue with this cause-effect sequence until you come back to where you started.
>
> What you see in front of you is a simplified version of what happened to thousands of towns and cities across the United States.

Systemic Relationships and Change

When students have a reasonably good grasp of all the pieces of the model, we can move on to the exploration of relationships. This is the point at which the applicability of the model to the traditional disciplines begins to be apparent. If we're interested in a religious movement, an architectural style, a technological innovation, a change in language, an increase in crime, a trend in literature, the implications of a decrease in energy supplies—whatever— the model says: What you're interested in is occurring within the context of one or more sociocultural systems. Here are forty-five or fifty other aspects of that system or those systems which may relate to what you're interested in. Some of the relationships will be absolutely essential to your understanding. Check them out. You'll be surprised at what you'll learn.

Here's an example of the sort of comprehensive assignment students can undertake once they have in mind all the pieces of the model:

> At one time, English vineyards regularly produced wine. Parts of the Near East which are now desert were once called the "Fertile Crescent." There were prosperous farms in Greenland.

> Earth's climate is constantly changing. (a) Study the available research and form a conclusion as to whether a cooling or warming trend is now more likely. (b) Using the model, speculate about the impact on your society if the decrease or increase during your lifetime is 1.5 degrees Celcius. (c) What policies, programs, and technologies would you recommend for minimizing the social impact of the climatic change?

> Obviously, you could work on this assignment indefinitely. We'll devote about twenty hours of class time to it, so pace yourselves accordingly.

> Use whatever format you like to present your work.

For obvious reasons, most of the illustrative activity I'm describing emphasizes content that is related to understanding the less-often-studied aspects of sociocultural systems. Here's an example of a very lengthy activity that places this kind of information in a somewhat secondary role:

> One way of thinking about Earth is to see it as a self-contained life support system. Air and water and other essentials of life are recycled and stored, ready to be used again. It's a good system. If taken care of, it seems capable of working for a very long time.

> One of the research concerns of the National Aeronautics and Space Agency is life-support systems. For travel away from Earth, what is needed are portable versions of Earth—systems which can supply food, water, air, and waste management for an indefinite period of time. To be practical in space, a self-contained

life support system would have to be light in weight, very small, and very energy efficient. However, in the much friendlier environment of Earth these factors are far less critical. The design problems for building a self-contained facility to provide a continuous supply of food, water, energy, and waste disposal would be challenging but not insurmountable. (If this seems far-fetched, remember that it's been done before. Not many decades ago, thousands of families had their own self-contained life support systems. They were bulky and required constant servicing by their owners, but they worked. They were called "family farms.")

(a) Design a self-contained life support system (SCLSS) sufficient to meet the needs of four people, operable anywhere, and needing no outside connections to utilities. Make it as compact as possible, so that it can be deliverable by truck or helicopter and adds relatively little to the size of a house.

(b) Compute the approximate cost per unit of the system.

(c) Devise a complete marketing program.

(d) Lay out multimedia advertising strategies.

(e) Predict both the possible and the probable impact of the equipment on the demographics, environment, patterns of action, and cognitive system of your society.

(f) Take and defend a value position on the *preferable* consequences of the equipment.

(g) Repeat (c) through (f) for another sociocultural system having a cultural heritage differing markedly from your own.

Here's another integrated assignment:

We've now assembled a model that directs our attention to four kinds of information about sociocultural systems—information about a system's demographics, about its environment, its important patterns of action, and its shared cultural premises. We've also broken these four general categories down into about forty-five subcategories of information.

With the other members of your team, generate questions which could help you analyze each of these subcategories as they apply to your age group.

For example, to learn about patterns for educating, you'd want to know the various kinds of information your society considers important for you to know, who usually has responsibility for teaching these kinds of information, at what age instruction usually begins, where it takes place, and so forth.

When you've completed the questions, (a) Answer them as they would be answered for a typical member of your society who is your age. (b) Locate several elderly individuals who are members of your society. Ask them the same questions you've asked yourself about each of the model components. Have them answer as they would have answered when they were your age, describing not so much their individual experience but what was typical at the time.

What kinds of changes, particularly in patterns of action and cultural premises, have taken place? Which of these changes do you consider important? Why?

And an activity I'd assign if I had the necessary resources:

Last term we used the model to take a very close look at the dominant segment of American society—middle-class America.

Because of its power to affect life in America, there is another society that Americans ought surely to understand as thoroughly as possible: the U.S.S.R.

The boxes on the table over there contain hundreds of pieces of data. You can think of them as typical "slices of life" in Moscow (except that all have been translated into English). There are newspaper articles, poems, papers written by schoolchildren, transcriptions of family and street small talk, wall posters, pages from textbooks, summaries of plots of popular movies, folklore, the budgets of individuals, families and the city, the words of rituals, favorite proverbs, popular songs, letters, descriptions of games, films of dances, pages of diaries, segments of novels, jokes, pictures of all kinds, maps, floor plans of houses, and much, much else.

Look at the data, talk about it, analyze it, argue about it. Then, using all the components of the model, profile that segment of Soviet society represented by the data.

Stay open and flexible. Don't begin writing immediately.

These activities and others I've used for illustrative purposes may not be viewed with enthusiasm by all educators. I acknowledge my lack of concern for the welfare of the traditional disciplines. I want to help students under-stand themselves, make sense of the world around them, and function in ways which increase their (and humankind's) chances of survival.

But if my assignments don't suit, that's no problem. The model can be used to generate instructional activities endlessly, activities which reflect the perspective of the humanities, language, the social or natural sciences, history, or anything else that belongs in the general education curriculum. It can encompass just about every teacher's favorite assignment. It excludes almost no lesson presently being taught (albeit suggesting that many aren't worth the effort).

The important thing is to recognize that the primary objective of general education is to expand our understanding of reality—a very complex reality. In the words of A. G. Afanassiyeff, "The world surrounding us consists not of separate things isolated from one another, but of a multitude of mutually bound and interacting objects—certain kinds of unified formations or wholenesses." We must recognize that the primary objective of general education is to expand understanding of reality; that, in our attempt to understand reality, sociocultural systems structure our perceptions; that sociocultural systems must therefore be understood; that, in order to understand sociocultural systems it is necessary to use a conceptual model; and that such a model, if it is comprehensive, will reflect our present level of understanding of the screen through which we view reality and of reality itself, and serve as a relatively simple and practical but comprehensive and powerful tool for selecting, organizing, and integrating the content of instruction bearing on that reality.

On such a theoretical foundation we could build a solid, sophisticated general education curriculum. We could have a curriculum that made of the information explosion a fascinating challenge rather than a threat to the status quo or a phenomenon to be ignored. We could have a curriculum that meshed with what is known about how the mind organizes knowledge. We could have a curriculum that moved decisions about the relative significance of various content into the realm of the rational. We could have a curriculum that gave to ourselves and our students the power and beauty of integrated knowledge. We could have a curriculum that wove the elements of general knowledge so tightly and efficiently together there would be more time for the specialization today's technologically-complex world demands. We could have a curriculum always and absolutely in touch with the moment and the era.

We could have all of that. But for a price: acceptance of the painful, threatening fact that the pictures of reality we now hold in our heads, and share with reassuring comfort with those around us, are inadequate for the task at hand.

Index

145